Nurture Yourself First

Gentle Steps in Personal and Planetary Transformation

Ilenya A. Marrin, DSS

BALBOA.
PRESS

A DIVISION OF HAY HOUSE

Passage from *Spiritual Warrior: The Art of Spiritual Living* by John-Roger and all other John-Roger quotes reprinted by permission of Peace Theological Seminary and College of Philosophy.

Kristin Neff's quote included by permission of the author.

Balboa Press books may be ordered through booksellers or by contacting:

Balboa Press
A Division of Hay House
1663 Liberty Drive
Bloomington, IN 47403
www.balboapress.com
1 (877) 407-4847

Because of the dynamic nature of the Internet, any web addresses or links contained in this book may have changed since publication and may no longer be valid. The views expressed in this work are solely those of the author and do not necessarily reflect the views of the publisher, and the publisher hereby disclaims any responsibility for them.

The author of this book does not dispense medical advice or prescribe the use of any technique as a form of treatment for physical, emotional, or medical problems without the advice of a physician, either directly or indirectly. The intent of the author is only to offer information of a general nature to help you in your quest for emotional and spiritual well-being. In the event you use any of the information in this book for yourself, which is your constitutional right, the author and the publisher assume no responsibility for your actions.

Cover art and author photo by Solara Rael Pastore.

Print information available on the last page.

ISBN: 978-1-5043-5497-4 (sc)
ISBN: 978-1-5043-5498-1 (hc)
ISBN: 978-1-5043-5499-8 (e)

Library of Congress Control Number: 2016905678

Balboa Press rev. date: 11/11/2017

Contents

I dedicate this book to my husband, Alf Marrin, and my parents, Donald and Kathleen Griffith, for the many lessons in loving and learning that they provided.

And to John-Roger and John Morton for their ever-present demonstration of loving, practical wisdom, and clarity of direction.

Acknowledgments

I gratefully acknowledge the following people whose lives have touched mine with shared learning, growth, and inspiration. These have left a lasting impression in my heart and soul.

Thanks to my beloved husband, Alf Marrin, and to my parents, Don and Kathleen Griffith; my brother, Don Griffith; and my sister, Roojeanne Hartel. Thanks to Dr. John-Roger and Dr. John Morton at Peace Theological Seminary and College of Philosophy for lessons of soul transcendence and practical spirituality, and to Drs. Ron and Mary Hulnick at the University of Santa Monica for their groundbreaking training in spiritual psychology.

Deep gratitude to dear friends who shared of themselves and their wisdom over several decades—Corryn Crosby-Muilenberg, Kiki Corbin, Robert Ball, Mary Ellen Chames, Lucrezia Covacevich Nelson, Dr. Martha McBride, Berti Klein, Virginia Schellberg, Lorraine Andrew, Cheryl des Montaignes, Cheryl Allen, Janet Graham, Dr. Michael Kudlas, Jae Kealing, Pat Halloran, Carol Mullins, Grant Overstake, Leora Wesling, Nancy Breth, Seti Walker, Patty Yoon, Whitley Quan, Lesley Crowell, Carol Jones, Karla Huber, Solara Pastore, and Kathy Ashford.

Thanks as well to all my other wonderful friends, clients and students who have taught me so much about human resilience and the power of loving and nurturing ourselves.

Introduction

My purpose in writing this book is to share information about self-nurturing, to sow seeds of love and wisdom from my experience, and to encourage women everywhere to grow these seeds in their own wonderful ways. Too often women take care of everyone but themselves, resulting in stress, burnout, or illness and diminished effectiveness. They lose the joy of living. Overwhelmed women need to give themselves the same compassion, encouragement, and support they so readily share with others. Taking care of yourself first is the foundation for healthy, authentic, effective living.

Nurture Yourself First for a Change is an invitation to take gentle steps in personal and planetary transformation.

I want women to experiment and discover their favorite ways to create more awareness of their own needs and to build inner trust, strength, and serenity. As each woman consistently practices self-compassion and self-care, she will bounce back from stress more easily, becoming a powerful force for solutions in both family and community.

Loving is the common denominator for humans around the planet. Love is often obscured by conflict, violence, terrorism, war, natural disasters, global warming, inequality of wealth, economic woes, and failing health care systems. Nevertheless, we are moving forward and creating a future. We must resolve challenges from neighborhoods to nations.

Our world struggles in a healing crisis. The resolution of this crisis will necessitate harmonious cooperation with diverse others and the nourishment of our planet. When enough ordinary women and men want to survive in peace, we will forge a much more accepting atmosphere—an atmosphere of living in loving that transcends ethnic, religious, and national boundaries.

My vision is that women around the world are caring for themselves as never before to bring forward their resilience and heart-centered wisdom as a steadying force in our global transition to an age of living love.

In the midst of this global healing crisis, the Western world is awash in self-help information. We have been inundated with advice on how to improve our lives. If you are like me, too often you learn about a great idea, try it for two days, and then let it slide away. Energy and interest fizzle in the face of daily demands and dramas. You might even turn those tips into sledgehammer *shoulds* to pound yourself down.

If you are tired of being sloshed around by life, tired of people pleasing, tired of stress and drama, I have one main tip to offer. *Take care of yourself first.*

This has been one of my biggest life lessons. If I take care of my essential aspects, I am happier, more effective, and more successful, and I am also able to give without depleting myself. I am resilient and able to rebound from challenges without undue stress. It comes down to loving myself and performing small, consistent actions to nurture, care for, and encourage myself. When I stick to a few supportive routines, my life expands. My energy picks up. I am creative, joyful, and loving. I am pleased, and my friends are amazed by my accomplishments. I feel clear about my purpose in life. I am in tune with myself and my God.

I'm sharing my story and key strategies so that you can also take care of yourself first. *Nurture yourself.* Then give to others from your overflowing abundance of loving energy.

Self-nurturing is the practical application of love. Small, simple, self-caring actions, taken consistently, bring love and healing to daily life, often transforming pain into celebration. Wherever you experience stress or criticism and judgment of your own process, you will find an easier way through gentle, encouraging, supportive steps that nurture your physical, emotional, mental, and spiritual levels of consciousness.

Having known severe stress and both physical and emotional pain, I share from experience. I was slow to learn self-nurturing because I locked into pushing and driving myself to perfection in helping others for years. After three decades of consciously working to love and nurture myself, I still experience disturbances, but I move through them much faster. What used to take weeks now takes days or even hours or minutes.

To help you plan your reading approach, I have listed sections of the book here. You might read *Nurture Yourself First for a Change* from cover to cover or read the first part and then pick the chapters that seem most relevant to your current needs. Write in the margins. Talk it over with friends. Adapt my suggestions to your needs and lifestyle. Keep asking yourself, "How can I make this work for me?"

Part 1: My Journey into Change is the story of my stress, health burnout, and wake-up call that led to learning to nurture myself consistently and profoundly.

Part 2: Nurture Yourself for a Change is an overview of self-nurturing, debunking the myth that taking care of yourself is selfish. Here, I also indicate how stress provides instant opportunities for better self-care and how taking care of you first can help you assist others.

Part 3: Nurturing Change, Six Simple Strategies provides six foundational tools for taking excellent care of yourself. Start your personal experiment in change with one or more of these.

Part 4: Fine-Tuning Change: More Strategies contains additional strategies for self-care that you can add when you are ready.

Part 5: Nurture Yourself and Keep the Change shows how to create your own simple self-nurturing plan and maintain your gains through a supportive lifestyle and circles of friends with similar goals.

Part 6: Nurture Yourself and Change the World is about your power as part of a global awakening into a greater loving consciousness.

Nurture Yourself First for a Change is filled with examples and a few of my favorite self-nurturing strategies. I also encourage you to discover your own methods for taking excellent care of yourself on all levels. Share your learning with friends and family members, and help spread the balm of self-nurturing!

Also, please share the results of your personal explorations and experiments in taking care of yourself first! Post on my blog, www.IlenyaMarrin.com, or follow my self-nurturing moments on Instagram (IlenyaMarrin) so we can enjoy the fun of learning and growing together! As much as time permits, I respond and interact online, and I love building our community of powerful women who are embracing self-nurturing lifestyles. Share your thoughts about challenges. Let us know of successful strategies and what you are learning about yourself. Ask questions, get answers, and help to inspire others.

PART 1

My Journey into Change

Take care of yourself
so you can help take care of others.
Don't hurt yourself,
and don't hurt others.
Use everything
for your learning, growth and upliftment.[1]
—John-Roger

After years of being an official helper, I desperately needed to learn to nurture myself for a change. The next two chapters detail my story and reveal some highlights from a few students who transformed crucial areas in their lives through self-nurturing.

Crashing and Crawling
into Self-Nurturing

*I finally asked the right question, "How can
I quit pushing and driving myself?"*

Illness Allowed Self-Nurturing

After college I became a child welfare social worker. I loved my work. Periodically, I had to go through court to remove badly neglected or abused children from their parents, which was extremely stressful. Invariably, I developed a chest infection that was obviously related to some emotional grief and my body's need for rest. I needed antibiotics and two or three days of rest. At home I slept, read, sewed, or embroidered, embracing quiet or mildly creative nurturing activities while my body recovered. Although I was sick several times a year, this program worked fairly well for quite a while.

Fast-forward past my two years of social work in London, my writer/editor/publicist career in Las Vegas, and my private practice as a psychotherapist in Tucson.

Stress and Chronic Illness

I worked once more in children's services, this time in a large county in California with some of the toughest assignments in the agency. I was responsible for children so emotionally disturbed that they could not live in family foster homes but needed round-the-clock professional supervision in group homes. Many had been in the system for years.

It was not easy, but I felt I was making a difference by helping children and families through some incredibly challenging situations.

One December morning, I was expecting a promotion to supervisor. Instead, we huddled in an impromptu staff meeting and learned that the county had declared bankruptcy. There would be no promotions. Hiring was frozen. I narrowly missed being laid off. Caseloads went up, but the client visits, case documentation, court reports, and court appearances still had to be completed. And I still got crisis calls in the middle of the night.

I did my best to manage it all. I met deadlines, saw my clients, wrote thorough reports to minimize time waiting in court, and juggled multiple crises daily.

My health went down the tubes. In the first fifteen months after the county bankruptcy, I took prescribed antibiotics thirteen times. I was never free of chest congestion and sinus infection. A chronic cough ruled my life. Many times a day in my cubicle or in meetings with clients or on the freeway, I doubled over and coughed for minutes. Eventually, I recovered from the spasm and carried on. I seldom took days off even when I was sick because catching up with missed work was impossible, and I could not expect my colleagues, who carried equally heavy workloads, to pick up the slack for me.

I continued to have neck pain because of whiplash and bulging discs from an auto accident a few years earlier. I developed carpal tunnel syndrome and wore a wrist brace. Tired and achy all over and never a sound sleeper, I could not get comfortable in bed. I spent hours awake in the dark, flopping around, imagining strategies to help my clients, rehearsing testimony or simply fretting over how to get everything done. Some days I started nodding off in traffic. Scary!

Mounting stress undermined my normally calm disposition. Many mornings I sobbed in the shower. There was not enough of me to go around. I felt my energy pouring down a black hole. Then I commuted an hour to my office, checked dozens of phone messages, and coughed my way through another round of calls, meetings, and client visits.

Cracking My Cosmic Egg

After about a year of this routine, I attended a weekend workshop on individual and world peace and had a revelation. For the first time, I saw how I sabotaged my inner peace by pushing and driving myself to excel. I was relentless, and my health was taking the hit.

Although excited by my new perception, I had no idea how to change my approach. Pushing and driving had been a part of me for so many years that I didn't realize I was doing it until that moment. On a break, I mentioned my stunning self-awareness to my husband, who said, "I've been trying to tell you that as long as I've known you." Yikes!

Next up in the workshop, a remarkable man named John-Roger, founder of the Movement of Spiritual Inner Awareness, educator, and author of more than fifty books, sat on a low stage and chatted with various participants. I raised my hand, eager to ask for suggestions on how I could be kinder to myself. He called on someone else. I laughed with the crowd as he talked with that person. But I really wanted to ask my question. He was looking around for the next person while I kept waving my hand. I was so enthusiastic that I jumped up and started down the aisle. He called on someone else, but he told me I was next. I sat down and enjoyed the discussion as the level of humor stepped up another notch. John-Roger had a gift for speaking to the heart that ranged from the sacred and profound to the hilarious in a moment.

At last, I walked to the microphone to ask my question. "How can I quit pushing and driving myself?"

"I don't think you can," said John-Roger.

My heart sank.

John-Roger turned to the audience and began cracking jokes. I listened and laughed too, and in a couple of minutes, he turned back to me.

"You through with your stuff now?" he asked.

My only thought was of a moment between my husband and me a few years ago. "All I can think to say is once when we lived in Tucson, Alf and I were having a big argument, and I was upset and crying. So he mooned me!"

Uproarious laughter!

John-Roger looked around for Alf, found him trying to hide at the back of the room, and led him by the hand to the stage.

"Did you really do that?"

With a red face, Alf nodded.

I added that I couldn't stay upset after the mooning. I had to laugh.

A psychology professor in the second row said, "A new conflict resolution skill."

For the next half an hour, J-R bantered with Alf and the audience about mooning and related silliness. I laughed until tears flowed.

Beginnings and Endings

Even though John-Roger never said a word directly about my issue, I left the workshop with a new awareness, a lighter heart, and an intention to stop pushing myself. I gradually began to nurture and care for myself.

I turned to a well-known holistic chiropractor and naturopath and stopped taking antibiotics. I stayed home for almost two weeks to rest and recover from my ongoing respiratory infection. I found a fabulous massage therapist in a medical doctor's office. That compassionate doctor referred me to a German-trained holistic doctor who helped assess and treat my fatigue. Then the doctor recommended a pulmonary specialist who diagnosed and began treating my asthmatic cough. After several tests ruled out other possibilities, I was diagnosed with chronic fatigue syndrome. My doctors recommended a disability leave.

I did not think a disability leave was a good idea. What would happen to my clients? Who would do my work?

A few months later, still struggling with recurring illness, chronic cough, ongoing fatigue, and pain, I agreed to partial disability status and worked part-time. I carefully orchestrated the transfer of many clients to other social workers. Even with holistic remedies and asthma medication, I was far from well.

My Wake-Up Call

That August I was still working part-time. My husband was away on business. My brother and his girlfriend were in town and stopped by for lunch. As usual, I felt slightly detached from reality, not connected with my body, just going through the motions.

I used my Wedgewood china, a relic from my first marriage, because I had not seen my brother in a long time and had never met his girlfriend. I dropped a plate. It shattered in the sink, but I made light of it. It was just a thing.

At some point during lunch, I put wet clothes and sneakers from the washer into the dryer. My little fifteen-year-old cat, Tukie-Bear, hopped in the dryer on top of the cold clothing. I shook my head. She was always exploring dark cupboards and corners. I left the door open and went on with my chores and the visit.

After lunch we decided to drive to the local grocery market. At the curb, I backed into my brother's car, leaving a dent in the front bumper. Fortunately, he was very understanding.

We returned to enjoy iced tea and dessert. They needed to leave. I stacked dishes in the sink, and when I passed the dryer, I shut the door and turned it on.

We stood outdoors, admiring bird-of-paradise flowers in the garden and saying our farewells. I was glad to see my brother and his girlfriend but relieved they were on their way. I was so exhausted. I went upstairs to nap.

At about nine that evening, I woke, went to the kitchen, and opened the dryer. I screamed. I called my neighbor and then my veterinarian. The neighbor drove me to the vet with a still-warm Tukie in my arms. I was devastated. I could scarcely think.

Everyone was so kind when I explained what happened. The neighbors drove me home and reluctantly left me when I said I would be all right. I called my husband at his hotel in St. Louis. He was marvelously kind and supportive.

I did not know what to do with myself. I had killed my favorite kitty in the whole world. I called a friend who listened with great compassion. At some point she reminded me to forgive myself. I said the words, but it was automatic. They were not getting in past my shock and pain. Eventually, I fell asleep.

The next day I went to work, but I was useless. I sat in the upstairs lobby with one or another of my colleagues, my spontaneous grief counselors. Our kind program manager walked through, saw my desolation, and asked what happened. "I killed my cat," I wailed.

From my caring colleagues, I finally got the message: I was under extreme stress, and I needed to rest and heal and take better care of myself. One friend gave me a ray of light when she suggested that my kitty sacrificed herself in order that I get the message to take care of myself before a major car accident or other serious event stopped me in my tracks.

Certainly not functional as a social worker at this point, I canceled immediate appointments and scheduled a meeting with my doctor for the next morning. I agreed to his previous suggestion—a full-time disability leave for three months.

I spent those next months vegetating. Many days I thought, *I really need to vacuum ... but not today.* I saw my doctors and followed their advice.

At Last, Nurturing Myself

At last, I put a supportive program in place. I did spiritual exercises (SEs) for one to two hours daily. Each day I listened to my own voice reading a fourteen-minute positive affirmation and to a healing meditation by John-Roger, focusing especially on the neck pain caused by bulging discs. When I had the energy, I wandered slowly on the beach. More often I perched on high rocks at the point in San Pedro and watched dramatic waves crash in and rush out. I sat at our kitchen table and sculpted small character doll heads from Super Sculpey or crafted greeting cards using scraps and found items. I haunted the library, devouring books about holistic health, nutrition, gentle exercise, simplicity, and frugality.

When the disability period ended, I resigned on medical advice. I had recovered enough to do something but not enough to return to a cauldron of stress. For the next eighteen months, I did part-time counseling and consulting work. I did not make much money, but I loved my work.

Two years later I went back to the county social services agency, but I was assigned to a different division. By this time I had learned to pace myself instead of driving myself to exhaustion. The county was out of bankruptcy and the agency had emerged as a leader in child welfare, even more proactive in helping families and children to reunite safely.

Eventually, I moved into the long-awaited supervisor position and loved nurturing and encouraging my dedicated staff. The work was intense, the challenges many, but I was seldom ill. I consciously orchestrated my days so I had quiet time to regenerate after long work hours.

Still Nurturing Me

Today I continue daily self-nurturing practices. Some have been valuable for years. I add new strategies and drop old ones as needed. Now I seldom get a cold and have had few full-fledged infections, all of which I treat with holistic products and spiritual approaches. In eighteen years, I have taken prescription antibiotics for a respiratory infection only once because it included a painful ear infection. I have steady energy and enthusiasm, and I seem to accomplish a lot through small steps that I take consistently. I am grateful for my life!

I continue to learn and grow when it comes to self-nurturing. Virtually every day I find new twists on caring for myself in my relationship with my husband, in my various social interactions, in home responsibilities, in creativity, and more. I still find plenty of opportunities to ask for what I need and to give myself what nurtures and supports me on many levels. Sometimes my growth opportunities are subtle, but other times they are head bangers. I do strive to have an attitude of loving for all these challenges as chances to expand my consciousness. Most of all, I intend to hold steady in loving myself, regardless of my activities or challenges.

My adventure continues. Please join me in learning the value of treating yourself as the amazing and worthy being that you are. When you take small steps repeatedly, taking care of yourself first, you can expect big changes to unfold over time. Wherever you are in your journey, I invite you to explore how self-nurturing can help you. Use my hard-won experience to avoid or to work your way out of overwhelming circumstances into self-compassion and resilience.

CHAPTER 2

The Self-Nurturing Project Is Born

*Best of all, my students' overwhelmingly
positive experiences inspired this book.*

My Portable Career

Around 2002, my husband's career path took us from
Southern California to suburban Detroit. Later, also for his
work, we moved to Burlington, Vermont, back to another
Detroit suburb, and finally to Wichita, Kansas. I did private
counseling and consulting, worked in a crisis-counseling
center, taught a college psychology class, and worked for the
University of Vermont in a program providing training for
Vermont social workers.

Our second stay in Detroit coincided with the downturn of the
US economy in 2008. I ended up teaching psychology at two
community colleges, where I loved interacting with students.

Though some were poorly prepared for college, many of my
students were eager to learn so that they could move into

adulthood and carve out careers. Others, laid off in midlife from manufacturing jobs, prepared for new careers. Young and old, most had personal questions about psychology. They longed to discover more about themselves. They asked the age-old questions, "Who am I? What is my purpose? What am I supposed to do with my life? How can I be happier, more peaceful, and less stressed? How can I have love when I have been so mistreated in my life up until now?"

Many were asking, "Why is life so unfair? Why am I always a victim?" Others were saying, "I believe in God, I think, but how does that work? I don't see much evidence of faith improving my life so far." Lots more said, "I want to change my life, but I don't know how."

I had a rich playing field!

The Self-Nurturing Project Is Born

In addition to highlights from the vast field of psychology, I needed to teach elements of critical or logical thinking. I fared poorly with the critical thinking assignments and term papers provided by the college. Perhaps because I did not create the assignments, I did not do a good job teaching them. My disappointment and frustration prodded me forward. At the first opportunity, I devised a self-nurturing project for students to use as the basis for their required term papers. Students had to create experiments, carry them out for five weeks, and thoroughly, logically analyze the results.

Each student chose at least one small strategy to support and encourage his or her own growth in each of three levels of consciousness—physical, emotional, and mental. As an option, they could include the spiritual level or create other categories, such as finances or creativity, for strategies that did not seem to fit in the main categories. My only rule was that the strategies for self-nurturing change had to be things the students wanted to do for themselves, not what parents, spouses, partners, or best friends said they should do!

When I carried home my first stack of term papers, awe, gratitude, and elation bubbled up. Students were getting it! Never mind their writing errors. They were making powerful, positive life changes through simple, consistent daily steps. They were energized, excited, and happy to be doing this project. Experiments may have started as another academic chore, but by the end, virtually all of the students reported remarkable learning as they assessed their five-week journey.

Student Stories

That first semester I recall a seventeen-year-old woman who started drinking eight glasses of water a day and reported being more alert during the day and sleeping better at night. Many students improved overall feelings of health and energy by choosing to cut out junk food and eat five fruits and veggies daily or by bringing healthy lunches and snacks for college and work. Others chose to eat breakfast regularly and noted better concentration during morning classes or jobs.

Many participants chose to exercise. Some walked their dogs or babies for fifteen minutes a day, and a few even ran six miles. Some worked out at a gym three or four days a week. Others did yoga or did a cardio workout. Typical reports included more energy, more confidence, better self-esteem, a little weight loss, and firmer muscles.

A professional fitness trainer who already worked out five hours a day switched one hour of bodybuilding for one hour of karate class and reported that the martial art reinvigorated his whole day. The joy of learning or perfecting moves he had not done in several years reenergized his outlook and made work more fun.

One young father started doing neglected yard work as a form of exercise, found that he loved gardening, and received plant starts from neighbors. Tending the yard shifted from a dreaded chore into a delightful break in his busy schedule.

A fifty-something woman spent fifteen minutes a day decluttering her home one corner at a time. She enjoyed the activity and the feeling of completion as each room took shape over the week, and she reported more self-confidence as a result of tackling this long-overdue project.

A twenty-something man switched his drive-time listening from rap to smooth jazz and reported being more peaceful and becoming much more respectful with the women in his life. He realized the latter change when several women pointed it out!

A sixteen-year-old girl researched anger management, stopped dramatic outbursts of anger with her family, and discovered that her father treated her with respect and that they could have adult conversations.

A twenty-one-year-old who worked two jobs in addition to a full class load practiced the "Mirror, Mirror" technique (chapter 18), quit her low-paying job, and used the additional time to study or have fun. Her grades and self-esteem both improved.

A middle-aged woman, still deeply grieving the death of her mother after ten years, forgave herself for judgments about issues between them. She made major progress in healing old wounds and finally accepted her mom's passing.

A young man who was not ready to say, "I love you," in the mirror instead looked at himself, flexed his muscles, and said, "I like you, dude! You're looking good!" He reported a wonderful boost in self-esteem and confidence!

A twenty-year-old, motivated by plans to attend a state university the following semester, increased his study habits. He began studying twenty-nine hours a week, and he noticed a predictable surge in his grades. He said, "I knew I wanted to be ready for a more rigorous academic life."

Many others increased study time from mere minutes to two or three hours per day, boosting grades and confidence. On my advice, one eighteen-year-old started using a dictionary while studying, and consequently, he improved his understanding and grades.

A hulking football player bought and used a day planner, suddenly taking control of his time and life. He noted improved grades and social relationships, and he gained a much more mature, responsible outlook.

Many students repeated positive affirmations or made up positive self-talk to challenge their negative tendencies.

An eighteen-year-old who was homeless, often sleeping in his car or on the couch of a different friend or relative each night, started daily listing of at least ten things he was grateful for, including safe shelter. Soon a step-grandmother made her couch available four nights a week, and his dad suddenly allowed this young man to stay over the other three nights—a big improvement that allowed for better self-care, work, and study habits.

A twenty-five-year-old mother of rambunctious two-year-old twins wanted to focus her experiment on changing their behavior. I suggested that rather than change the twins, she focus on giving herself permission to set boundaries for her energetic sons. Before starting her experiment, she thought that denying the boys their wishes meant she did not love them. To nurture new beliefs, she affirmed things like, "It's okay to say no," and, "I love myself enough to set limits for my kids." By the end of five weeks, she gleefully reported much more confidence as a person and a mother, and yes, she saw better behavior from the boys. She nurtured herself into a more proactive role as a mom, and the boys responded beautifully.

A thirty-year-old man repeated statements about saving money, and he was well on his way to affording his first real vacation by the end of the project.

A thirty-five-year-old wife and mother wrote down every penny she spent, discovered how she was overspending, and then created and followed a budget that allowed her to save for contingencies. She reported great relief with fewer financial emergencies, more self-confidence and self-trust, and a happier husband!

More than one student stopped smoking because of this project. When I casually commented about how hard it is to give up cigarettes to a young woman in the midst of changing this habit, she darted a glance at me and said, "I don't smoke cigarettes." I do not know how many gave up nicotine as opposed to other substances!

These are just a few quick highlights. Over more than four years at two colleges, about eight hundred students reported enthusiastically on this self-nurturing assignment. Typical comments included the following: "I learned to love myself." "I learned that if I want to, I can do anything." Best of all, my students' overwhelmingly positive experiences inspired this book.

PART 2

Nurture Yourself for a Change

Do you typically put yourself last when dealing with family and friends? Do you frequently assist others only to find yourself exhausted and overwhelmed? Do you take on extra projects, push yourself to perfection, and then crash into a cold or backache in order to recover?

What would happen if you took care of those other folks *after* taking care of yourself? What would happen if you made sure you were in excellent shape, balanced, and healthy on all levels so that you could easily and joyfully share with others?

What would change inside of you if you nurtured yourself?

CHAPTER 3

Are You Ready for Change?

*I hereby give you permission to nurture
yourself first for a change!*

Tools, Power, and Permission

You are a complex human being with many beautiful and sometimes contrasting personality aspects—wisdom and foolishness, creativity and monotony, independence and dependency, cooperation and rebellion, boldness and anxiety. Plus you have many layers or levels of consciousness, including physical, emotional, mental, and spiritual.

What if you knew you could transform your life by taking good care of your multidimensional self? What if you accepted that through nurturing and supporting yourself, you could more effectively assist others and even help to transform our world?

I am sharing some tools. You have the power to use them. I hereby give you permission to nurture yourself *first* for a change!

What Exactly Is Self-Nurturing?

Self-nurturing means taking great care of yourself on multiple levels. You actually know quite a lot about nurturing already.

You know how to be a good friend and listen, how to offer encouragement and assistance. You give tremendously to support your partner or spouse, your children, and possibly your parents. You support others at work and in your social circles. You have likely volunteered many times. You have helped heal bruises to little bodies and big egos, and you have helped to solve a great many practical problems, helping to facilitate the flow of life and love in your immediate world.

Let's take a deeper look.

Nurturing involves kindness and compassion as you help someone or something to thrive and grow. You provide encouragement, inspiration, and loving acceptance, the nutrients for healthy growth. You don't interfere, but you support the unfolding elements of growth. You encourage and celebrate each next step, however shaky. You go on observing, accepting, and loving as the blossom sprouts wings and takes flight!

Do you recognize this process?

Self-nurturing means applying these principles to yourself. With self-nurturing, you compassionately accept yourself as you are and make gentle, gradual changes, encouraging, supporting, and celebrating your growth. You discover and build core strength with simple practices of your choice, physically, emotionally, mentally, and spiritually. When you make changes on one of these levels, amazingly, the other levels also start to shift in a positive direction. As a result, over time, you begin to weather the storms of life with an inner acceptance and flexibility. Life becomes an adventure.

Why Nurture Yourself First?

I suggested earlier that through self-nurturing, you can transform your life, assist others more effectively, and even help change our world for the better. Let's take a closer look at these possibilities.

Transform Your Life

First, if you don't take care of yourself, who will?

When you are down on yourself or neglecting yourself, you might get a little sympathy or good advice. People will say, "You should—" But no one does the work to change your inner dynamics except you. You might receive gifts to help you through a tight spot. But what will prevent these situations from cropping up over and over again until you take care of yourself enough to face and learn from the root causes?

Ironically, I have found the root causes are almost always inside of me, and they respond beautifully to my simple, consistent self-nurturing approaches. If I nurture me, it is much easier to see options and act wisely to resolve my issues.

From Self-Compassion to Resilience

My old rule was, "To stay safe, try to be in control." My current guideline is, "Love myself no matter what." Since it is impossible to be in control of anything beyond my own skin and often darn hard to manage even that much real estate, loving myself no matter what is a lot more doable.

When you consistently take care of yourself, you also demonstrate self-compassion and develop greater resilience or ability to bounce back after a stressful event. With self-compassion, you naturally move to a place of observing and acknowledging *but not judging* aspects of yourself that might appear negative, limited, or lacking in some way. You practice empathy, and extend caring to yourself just as you do with others who are struggling or in pain. You shine the sunlight of understanding and acceptance onto your own marvelous work-in-progress self. This level of acceptance without judgment allows you to recover from challenges with more ease and grace.

Dr. Kristin Neff, a research psychologist at the University of Texas, Austin, has done groundbreaking research on self-compassion. Neff says, "Research indicates that in comparison to self-esteem, self-compassion is associated with greater emotional resilience, more accurate self-concepts, more caring relationship behavior, as well as less narcissism and reactive anger."[2] Connecting the practice of self-compassion with more resilience or the ability to bounce back from setbacks and challenges, she suggests that in the future, many may view self-compassion as more important than self-esteem.

A Cascade of Positive Effects

When you nurture yourself consistently, a cascade of positive effects may unfold.

- You drink in your gift of kindness and discover self-compassion.
- You enjoy immediate benefits in health and well-being on whatever level you apply the nurturing (physical, emotional, mental, or spiritual).
- You increase self-acceptance, self-confidence, self-worth, and self-trust.
- You build resilience and cope better with stress.
- You feel fulfilled and overflowing with loving energy, and you are able to share and assist others without depleting yourself.
- You become a model of excellent self-care, which encourages others to nurture themselves.

Self-nurturing is simple stuff that I have used to rework my approach to living. It took me a long time to get where I am, and I still must work to remain conscious and nurture myself daily. So this is not a quick fix. It is a gentle approach to self-transformation. The good news is that if I fall off my track, I simply get back on—thousands of times if need be. You can too.

This material is not new, but your inner results can be new every day. Use this information as a springboard for diving into life from a new angle. Upgrade your life experience. Brainstorm to create self-nurturing strategies adapted to your needs. Experiment.

Create self-nurturing success by consistently taking small steps. There's no need to be Superwoman! Do what you need to do and keep chalking up one small success after another until you reach your goal. If you are consistent with small steps, if you keep returning to these practices, you may be surprised to discover that you are living from the inside out, that you are responding to challenges rather than reacting to crises, and that you enjoy more vibrant loving, peace, and joy through all your daily ups and downs.

CHAPTER 4

Self-Nurturing Is Not Selfish

When you focus on your needs, your own learning, your purpose, and your direction, you keep your inner wellspring cleaned out, bubbling with clear loving energy. You have ample loving for yourself with plenty to share.

As you have read, did you find yourself thinking, *All this focus on self is too selfish*? Did you think, *I can't do that. I've always been told to put others first*?

Consider this. Self-nurturing is not selfish in any negative sense. It does not make you unspiritual, sinful, or narcissistic.

Better Boundaries, Less People Pleasing

Self-nurturing *does* make you less susceptible to the emotional and mental manipulations of unconscious, needy people who would love to have you do their work for them. As you learn to take good care of yourself, you might quit trying to rescue, fix, or control others. Self-nurturing empowers you to let your spouse, children, and coworkers learn their own lessons.

When you are in good shape because of self-nurturing, it is easier to hold your boundaries. You have less need to please others at your own expense. You can let them learn from their circumstances, mistakes, or the consequences of their choices, while you keep your eye on your own goals and direction. You are not against them. You love them enough to let them learn in their chosen ways. You love yourself enough to stick to your purpose and plan.

One thirty-something mom—I'll call her Emmy—found her husband's siblings in her home almost daily, hogging the television and helping themselves to food meant for her three young kids. Emmy's hardworking husband seemed unable to tell them no. As part of her self-nurturing project, Emmy told herself, "I'm taking care of myself and my family." Emmy told her in-laws they were not welcome to drop in. She changed the locks, and she refused to open the door to these freeloaders, who now had to rely on their own efforts and earnings. Within a week they stopped knocking, and Emmy's budget and temperament relaxed. Her "too nice" husband sighed with relief and thanked her for protecting their family. As Emmy discovered power to set boundaries, her confidence and self-worth soared.

Giving from Your Overflow of Loving Energy

Self-nurturing frees you to be more of who you really are and to live from your loving heart with compassion for others as well as yourself. Ultimately, you have more to share with others. When you focus on your needs, you keep your inner wellspring cleaned out, bubbling with clear loving energy. It is easier to focus on your own learning, goals, purpose, and direction. You have ample loving for you and plenty to share.

You give others freedom to live as they wish, making and learning from their mistakes just as you learn from yours! Of course, you care for children until they are old enough to care for themselves, but you don't take on other people's problems. Because you focus on your needs *first*, you no longer live in drudgery and resentment. As your cup runs over because of self-nurturing, you unlock a natural outflow of love, peace, and joy. You encourage and inspire all ages to see their next steps and find the strength to handle their issues themselves.

Even Helping to Change the World

When you take care of yourself, you become a transformative force in your family, workplace, and community. Your presence creates a rippling shift to calmer, more positive, and more creative perspectives. You stand in your own loving strength, sharing openly, encouraging others to be the strong and beautiful beings that they truly are. You might also begin to notice changes as your immediate family and friends make similar small changes or as you find new friends!

Take a moment and imagine what could happen if you truly nurture yourself for ten years. During each of those years, you casually influence just four people to be more nurturing of themselves, and each of them influences four others and so on down the line.

I did some simple math (see Math Chart: Ripples of Self-Nurturing in the end matter.) If each new nurturing person influences four more, in ten years your *first year* of personal self-nurturing could spread gently to help 1,398,100 people be less frenetic and frazzled! If you influence four new people each additional year and they spread self-nurturing to four more each and so on, you may potentially influence at least 1,864,120 people.

If even a thousand of you reading this book learn to nurture yourselves consistently and then encourage other women to take better care of themselves, we will enjoy a lovely cultural shift to a more responsible, healthy, authentic, and loving lifestyle.

CHAPTER 5

Stress: An Opportunity for Self-Nurturing

Stress is the teacher.

I see an epidemic of stress, frustration, worry, and pain affecting individuals, families, and communities. Young people fret about the future, struggling to get educations, start careers, and pursue their dreams. Adults scramble to maintain financial balance at great cost to personal and family life, often while taking care of both younger and older generations. Health, wealth, and happiness diminish as the cost and effort of living rises. Foundations of inner peace and purpose erode in a flood of demands to cope ... or else!

Every day stress nibbles away at your sense of self. Major events only make things worse. Typically, you judge the pain or stress plus the situation that triggered it. You might use a lot of energy trying to ignore or to control the painful situation. You might look like you are fighting and resisting or just the opposite, trying to rescue, help, or fix situations or people. In either case, you miss inner peace and harmony. Do you recognize any of these patterns?

My favorite way to short-circuit these self-defeating cycles is with self-nurturing.

I have learned that we can never really control the experience of pain because we cannot control the people or situations around us. All we can control is our inner response and our own behavior. Do we react with knee-jerk emotions and defensive or blaming thoughts, or do we respond in a balanced way from the depth of heart and soul? I find peace when I nurture myself enough that I can respond from heart and soul.

Stress Is Not the Problem

Stress is not the problem. Whether quiet and subtle or loud and obvious, stress is the teacher. It is both a symptom and an opportunity as well as an invitation for self-nurturing. It says, "Something here is not working. Find a better way."

Challenges will always touch your life. Kids fail. Loved ones get sick or pass away. Health issues develop. Jobs go away. Stressful new jobs appear. Families move, come together, and/or split up. The economy bounces around, and politicians change our rules. Self-nurturing helps you bounce back from these challenges as well as daily hassles.

When we persist in compassionate self-care, we naturally use the inevitable stress to help us correct many issues, including our own attitudes. We grow, enjoy more inner peace, and advance as happy, creative beings. We can love and be loved, starting with our own sweet selves. We can share an abundance of love with others, building healthy families and a more peaceful world.

As a powerful antidote to our epidemic of stress-related issues, I propose applying self-nurturing on an individual basis.

PART 3

Nurturing Change:
Six Simple Strategies

Why try to jump across a ditch and risk falling flat when baby steps will take you down the grassy slope and back up again more surely?

Gentle! Fun! Easy?

This section offers gentle, often fun foundations for self-nurturing, but you might write them off as simplistic or boring. Persisting is not easy!

Regular practice yields great results. *Take very small steps consistently.*

Your desire for transformation, willingness to change, plus *consistent* self-nurturing action steps will be keys to success. For now, look for a few strategies to fit your needs. Soon you will be a compassionate experimenter, creating and learning from your own self-nurturing routines.

CHAPTER 6

My Spiritual Insurance Clause

I may wish for specific outcomes for myself or loved ones,
but I really want whatever is ultimately highest and best.

The Light Prayer

As a huge aid to self-nurturing, I often use my favorite short prayer, "Light for the highest good of all concerned,"[3] which I learned from John-Roger. Many times I make it even shorter and simply say, "Light!" I am referring to the light of God or the Christ, but you might think of this light in the context of your own faith or philosophy as the highest, purest, most loving essence in the universe.

(Please note that throughout this book, I use the word God as a term that most people understand, but feel free to substitute whatever word or words work for you, such as Divine Creator, Source, Infinite Spirit, Higher Power, etc.)

I sometimes think of this Light prayer as my spiritual insurance clause. I may wish for a specific outcome for myself or loved ones, but I really want whatever is ultimately highest and best. So as I hold intentions or offer prayers or blessings, I include a request that all unfold "in the light for the highest good." This means that if what I personally want is not for the best, I am willing to let it go in favor of whatever is truly for the best. I say this prayer and do my best to let it go, leaving my request in God's hands and trusting that all does indeed work out for the highest good.

I actually say the shorter form of this prayer, "Light," very often throughout the day—when I drop a fork, when I trip on a sleeping dog in the dark, when I feel irritated with my husband, or when I'm working through endless phone prompts and trying to reach a live person. Hundreds of daily hassles—all the stuff that is not the way I want it to be—find me saying silently or out loud, "Light!"

It helps me remember that better outcomes are possible and that I do not need to "be in control." I simply need to accept what is present and work with it as best I can. I can walk away, crawl over, duck under, go around, and cooperate or not. Each obstacle offers a choice point that I can place in the light. I can choose to stay neutral and observe with as much loving as I can muster, or I can dive into anxiety and irritation. Which is more fun? Which is more loving toward myself? More light helps a lot!

I offer this as a simple but profound way of creating greater alignment between your practical daily life and your spiritual life. Using this prayer in preparation for my own self-nurturing processes is powerful. If nothing else, it reminds me many times a day of my intention to cooperate with God's will or the divine essence flowing through my life. You might want to incorporate this or similar words that fit easily for you with your own faith practices.

CHAPTER 7

The Neutral Loving Observer

*As you experiment, neutrally and lovingly
observe your self-nurturing process.*

Have you wished for more balance and poise in your life? Are you fed up with scrambling through one hassle after another? Do new challenges throw you into a frustration fit? Do little things trigger undue anger or anxiety?

Being a neutral loving observer (NLO) is a foundation for self-nurturing. When you gently, compassionately, and scientifically observe, challenging situations and other people's opinions no longer push you around. Instead you watch your own process! As an NLO, you stay calmer and see more solutions because you skip getting caught in a dozen dramas a day.

Discovery

I stumbled into being a neutral loving observer rather haphazardly in the midst of my stress and health challenges.

I noticed that when the hassles were upon me and I felt most stressed, in those rare moments when I stayed neutral, I had much better results. I did not waste time with being emotionally upset. I simply observed and aimed for corrective actions. I noticed that at the best of times, I also did not judge myself or the other folks involved.

As I gradually chose this approach more consciously, I immediately noticed fewer self-judgments in small daily frustrations. When I did judge myself or the situation, I moved to forgiveness (explained in the next chapter) of my self-criticisms more quickly. *Then I could correct the problem and move on with more serenity.*

I first articulated this NLO approach during my doctoral studies in spiritual science. By then I loved the idea of bringing scientific objectivity to the consideration of my own life, but I still found it easy to slide from logical observation to the harsh observation of my ancient inner critic.

When I consciously added an element of loving, I created a new level of observation. I watched myself from a higher altitude, at times one of infinite compassion, even while noting the dumb, dorky things I thought or did. As a side effect, I became more compassionate and accepting with others, and yet I took better care of myself, not letting people step on my toes. Gradually, I learned to maintain my NLO perspective through tense situations and larger conflicts. By holding in neutrality and a quiet loving attitude, not judging but rather simply watching, I stayed peaceful and resolved issues with more grace and ease.

Dirty Dishes and Chinese Takeout

I knew I was onto something after a few months of consciously practicing as the NLO. I returned from a weeklong visit with my mother in Texas. The Super Shuttle pulled up in front of our apartment, and I mustered my last bit of travel energy to get my over packed suitcase indoors. I was oh-so-ready for the nurturing of my own orderly and familiar surroundings! I dropped my jacket on the bannister, gave my husband a kiss, and went to grab a glass of water from the kitchen. Uh-oh! I gazed upon dozens of haphazardly stacked dirty dishes, pots, and pans all over our small kitchen.

Previously, I would have felt instant irritation, quickly quashed those judgments and feelings, but erupted an hour later with resentment, criticizing and complaining. We would have had a big argument, and I probably would have cleaned the kitchen myself, still irritated.

Instead, practicing as the neutral loving observer, I got my glass of water. As I lugged my suitcase upstairs, I calmly commented, "Obviously, the mess in the kitchen is not mine. Let's order Chinese takeout for dinner." My husband promptly agreed, and a few minutes later, he came up to apologize for the mess. I stayed out of the kitchen all evening. We enjoyed our General Hso orange chicken and spring rolls in the living room. The next day when I got home from work a little late, he was scrubbing the last of the pans and putting them away. No drama, no pain. Wow. Being an NLO worked a small miracle!

Be a Neutral Loving Observer.

Ever since you started exploring as a toddler, you have been a kind of scientist, figuring out what works. Today you can create a scientific self-nurturing game, a laboratory-of-life adventure as a neutral loving observer of yourself and your world.

To become a neutral loving observer, you will simply practice a bit of scientific observation with objectivity or neutrality, plus compassion for yourself. In other words, you can practice neutral loving observation with three inner action steps.

- Observe.
- Stay neutral.
- Bring in the loving.

Begin with small daily experiences, and you will gradually learn to observe yourself in more complex, emotionally intense situations. Try it.

Observe.

Pause and check inwardly. What is going on for you in this moment? Look, listen, and feel. What are you perceiving, feeling, or telling yourself? You already observe situations and people around you. Now observe yourself too. Consciously watch your actions and reactions.

If you find yourself saying, "Oh, there I go again," "I really did a good job in that little interaction," or, "I sure seem out of balance this morning," you are observing yourself. Noticing your state of being in the moment is about staying conscious of your actions, motivations, body sensations, emotions, thoughts and flashes of intuitive knowing. At first, you are "taking a snapshot," but practice will help you sustain self-observation for longer periods as you wish.

Stay Neutral.

Keep your observations objective. Be a loving, curious scientist. Do not immediately interpret what is going on. Do not jump to conclusions about other people or yourself. Just watch and listen. Pay attention. Look. Listen. Notice. If you find that you are second-guessing yourself or saying you "should" have done or said something differently, you are subtly judging yourself. That is not neutral!

To move to neutral, try restating your observation as a description. Let's say I just broke the toaster. Frustrated, I could say, "I shouldn't have twisted that knob so hard!" Where do my thoughts go next after this judgment? My old reflexive patterns would urge me to cuss in my head a little and feel that I'm bad in some way (stupid, clumsy, unconscious) and deserve punishment. Some years ago something like this could throw me off balance for hours.

What happens inwardly if instead I neutrally describe what happened? "Yikes! I twisted that knob so hard it broke off." My NLO thinking then says, "What a surprise! I didn't realize I was exerting that much force or that the knob was that fragile. Darn! I will need to do without or get a new toaster. Guess I will make toast in the broiler today."

A few minutes of disappointment and problem solving seems much easier on the inner me than judgment and guilt.

Another way to stay neutral is to restate your inner comment. "Next time I could do that a little differently." You might notice that such a simple reframing of your perspective brings a feeling of lightness and relief. Even a subtle judgment lifted usually feels lighter and brighter. To release larger self-judgments, use the powerful technique of self-forgiveness that I share in chapters 8 and 20, and see chapter 15, Nurturing Positive Focus through Language.

Bring in the Loving.

This is about extending loving to your own beautiful self the way you give it to your loved ones!

You might imagine yourself as a being of higher order, observing yourself in action. Pretend you are an angel watching over yourself. Or recall the most loving, accepting person you know, and ask yourself how he or she would view your current situation. Feel the great compassion as this being observes your process of learning and growing. Move into that being of higher order and love yourself unconditionally.

Experiment with observing yourself as if you were a young child, eagerly learning from every mistake and success. What compassion would you feel for a youngster who is exploring and growing through trial and error? Be the neutral loving observer and give that compassion, caring, and encouragement to yourself. Simply watch with love.

Practice gently.

Nurturing Yourself as a Neutral Loving Observer

As you experiment, neutrally and lovingly observe your self-nurturing process. Remind yourself a few times a day to observe your inner state of being. Ask yourself the following questions: *How* are you doing things? *What* are you thinking and feeling? Sticky notes or phone reminders might help you focus on this.

When you practice your self-nurturing strategies, observe any changes in your behavior, emotions, moods, confidence, self-esteem, self-perceptions, self-talk, and spiritual experiences. To maintain your NLO stance, note interesting results as you go along. Perhaps spend five minutes before bedtime capturing your observations of the day.

I now find being an NLO is a mind-set for successful daily living. The more I use it, the more smoothly my life flows. When I succeed as a neutral loving observer, I accept what is present, enjoy inner peace, and stay calm under stress. Staying peaceful and centered means that in any moment I can see more options available for next steps. I am open to a broader perspective than I would be if I were irritated, impatient, or judgmental. As a caring, compassionate observer of my own life, I give myself freedom to learn, grow, and live more and more from my authentic self.

If you do nothing else to nurture yourself, practice neutral loving observation.

CHAPTER 8

Self-Forgiveness

How have you judged yourself today?
What would your life be like if you dropped the judgments?

Witnessing Self-Forgiveness

A friend now long deceased once called me when he was extremely anxious about a medical procedure. He had an appointment three days later to clear blockages in his painful prostate gland, which had swollen to the size of a softball. I asked for "light for the highest good" and suggested that we seek spiritual assistance according to his faith.

As we talked, this man revealed deep shame about his childhood when his mother physically, emotionally, and sexually abused him. His father did not intervene. As an adult, he became promiscuous and disrespectful of women. Now on a journey of spiritual awakening, he felt profound guilt and remorse.

I suggested the process of self-forgiveness, and for perhaps fifteen minutes, he quietly and sincerely made statements about forgiving his judgments of incidents from decades earlier. He forgave himself for judging his parents, for somehow unconsciously attracting or allowing those abusive experiences, for his own sexual excesses, and for judging himself relentlessly. When his self-forgiveness process seemed complete, he sounded much more balanced and accepting of his upcoming medical treatment.

The next morning he called again, gleeful. Overnight, his prostate had shrunk back to normal! He kept the doctor's appointment as a precaution, but everything was fine.

Six years later his prostate was badly swollen, and once more, a phone consult and a healthy dose of self-forgiveness put things right. My friend's intention to forgive himself opened space for divine assistance and restorative action. When we forgive ourselves, there is room for miracles. That is the power of self-forgiveness in a spiritual context.

Thanks to the University of Santa Monica

I first learned about self-forgiveness in 1986 at the University of Santa Monica (USM). Thank you, Drs. Ron and Mary Hulnick, directors of USM! Applying self-forgiveness to my own issues thousands of times has freed me from heaps of minor self-criticisms as well as ancient, largely unconscious, and hugely emotional self-judgments. My clients and students regularly demonstrate the power of self-forgiveness. Consciousness shifts profoundly. If you feel stuck, confused, ashamed, guilty, embarrassed, worried, angry, or anxious, if you are blaming others, putting yourself down, or experiencing any other negative emotions or thoughts, you have an opportunity for self-forgiveness.

Self-Judgments: Excess Baggage

Let's look first at a universal human challenge. Self-judgments conflict directly with self-nurturing. In addition to blatant "How stupid of me!" or "I could just die of the shame" feelings, self-judgments sneak around as subtle words and half-formed thoughts. Behind your fatigue, depression, stress, and anxiety lurk dozens of self-judgments that can drag you down. Chances are that you have no clue how deeply and how often you judge yourself.

Both obvious and stealthy judgments act like excess baggage you drag along. You pull extra weight, move forward awkwardly, and get stuck at critical turning points. To bolster your sense of worth and esteem, you spend valuable energy keeping these judgments "in their place," tucked away in back corners of your consciousness.

"So what?" you may ask. "I'm getting along pretty well."

You are a student of life here on earth to learn and grow. The nature of learning includes mistakes. Unfortunately, if you are like most folks, you judge your mistakes. "I shouldn't have done that. I'm a terrible person for saying that."

It is challenging enough that you frequently make missteps, mistakes, and miscommunications. Heaping judgments on your head compounds your misery. Why keep doing that?

Self-judgments *might* point to a problem you need to correct. Do they help you step forward in love, peace, and joy? Do the self-incriminations increase your health and well-being or your success on any level? Not that I can see.

Why not take a self-nurturing approach? Simply correct any error and move forward without the excess baggage. You could look at your mistake, make amends as needed, and move forward with a plan to do better next time.

Consider the following two questions:

- How have you judged yourself today?
- What would your life be like if you dropped the judgments?

Why Use Self-Forgiveness?

Self-forgiveness is a remarkable tool for self-nurturing.

- Self-forgiveness allows you to release whatever stands between you and your authentic self, between you and the experience of greater love, peace, and joy.
- Self-forgiveness frees emotional energy that may have been stuck for years, creating inner freedom and room for more creativity and success.
- Self-forgiveness allows you to accept and love yourself as you are with compassion for your human process of learning and growing.

Ilenya A. Marrin, DSS

Four Keys for Nurturing Past Self-Judgments

1. **Neutral Loving Observation.** Notice your self-judgments. *Oh, there I go again, shoulding. Hmm, I just put myself down. Wow, that thought was pretty self-critical.* Also notice when you simply observe and do not judge but stay neutral and accepting of yourself. Wonderful!
2. **Acceptance.** Skip the judgments entirely. Accept and love yourself as you are—even your mistakes and flaws. Certainly, continue to focus on improving, but see yourself as a work in progress. Love your process of learning by trial and error. The opposite of self-judgment is self-acceptance. When you accept yourself, you need no self-forgiveness. But when you judge, self-forgiveness is the antidote.
3. **Self-Forgiveness.** When you notice you are judging yourself, consciously forgive yourself as quickly as possible. However you do it, forgive and forget. Let go of the self-judgments.
4. **Self-Compassion.** In the spaces where judgments used to exist, place your loving and self-compassion. Focus on nurturing and growing positive, healing qualities. Return to acceptance.

When you are ready for more, check out chapter 20, "Self-Forgiveness: Moving Deeper."

CHAPTER 9

Listen for the Loving

Listening within creates a clear space
for loving awareness to emerge.

What would happen if you gave the gift of deep listening to your inner self? What would come present if you listened with loving and compassion to your own needs and desires? What resolution and completion might occur if you allowed yourself to be aware of your inner wisdom?

Listen. Listen to yourself, tuning in to your own needs. Listen to the silence, attuning yourself to the transcendental. Inner listening is one way to access intuition and creativity, and it is a big key for self-nurturing.

Many people do not know how to listen at all, much less to their own needs.

The Gift of Listening

In my classes I demonstrated with a simple exercise between partners. Taking turns, one student was to talk for a minute about any situation of his or her choice, and the other was supposed to listen for the full minute without speaking. Most students found it uncomfortable to talk and almost impossible to listen silently for sixty seconds. We discussed how hard it is to listen when we are busy thinking of our responses and when we are accustomed to switching back and forth every few seconds in a conversation.

We also talked about the gift of listening to another. Students shared how wonderful they felt on those rare occasions when another truly heard them. Being a good listener is one of the greatest gifts you can give to a friend or family member. Many will consider you wise and caring. You might also find that listening deeply to others, paying attention, and not interrupting helps you learn to be present with yourself.

Listening to Word Salad

I once listened intently to a haggard, distressed, thirtyish woman—I'll call her Caitlin—whose long history of drug abuse had cost her dearly. Taking her preferred drug just before our conversation, Caitlin might have been speaking Martian. Except for occasional names, I heard a garbled word salad. Yet I knew she was sharing a meaningful story by her pauses and inflections, animated face, soulful eyes, and occasional tears. I held eye contact and listened. When she looked to me for a response, I said a compassionate "Oh" or "Uh-huh." After two and a half hours, she wrapped up, gave me a hug, and said good-bye.

By chance I saw Caitlin again two years later. She seemed brighter, more articulate, and much younger, and she thanked me for changing her life. She explained that she found the courage to start a new, drug-free chapter in her journey because of me. I must have looked quite puzzled. She said, "You are the only person who ever *really listened to my story.*"

If my listening *without understanding a thing* could help a person to turn her life around, what can your listening do? What if you started by listening for two minutes a day to your own self?

Listening to Yourself Is Nurturing Yourself

Inner listening is a natural healing process. It is a way of being with yourself and letting answers emerge from the depth of heart and soul.

If you were nurturing a young child, would you listen empathically to her concerns? Would you ask a few questions to draw her out and clarify?

Be the neutral loving observer in a listening mode. Practice listening to others, remaining silent but attentive until they are clearly ready for you to speak.

Practice listening to yourself the same way you would listen to another. Gently be present, and listen to your innermost thoughts and feelings. Do not argue with yourself or override unwelcome thoughts. Just listen. What you gain is precious awareness and understanding, fundamental elements in healing, renewing, or lifting consciousness.

Grieving the recent loss of her husband, Penny spoke to me about the value of listening within. Despite her sorrow she finds peace and even joy as she stills her active mind and listens deeply to the silence or the quieter thoughts that emerge from her consciousness. She acknowledges and then listens past whatever feelings of grief and anger arise. Listening to her own inner self helps her move through the pain and into acceptance of her loss.

Listening with Discernment

After some practice at inner listening, you might develop discernment in order to tell which inner voices are which. No, I do not mean that we are all hallucinating in the sense of mental illness! But I remember how I used to experience an inner hodgepodge of remembered voices (critical or praising parents and teachers), fragments of my own personality (rebellious teenager, daredevil, or wallflower), and conflicting conscious and subconscious aspects ("I want to" as opposed to "I shouldn't/couldn't"). Then there were random thoughts on the airwaves that were probably just floating through the atmosphere or vaguely recalled fragments from television or movies, but they weren't really mine. Somewhere in the midst of all that was my still, small voice offering profound wisdom when I needed it most. I had plenty of junk to clear away to hear my inner wisdom!

About a year into my original practice of meditating, I gained a profound lesson in listening with discernment. I heard an inner voice say, "Your mother is dying." Dismayed, I jerked out of my meditative state. After a few minutes of panic, I dialed home. My mother answered, and she sounded totally normal. I was so shocked, relieved, and embarrassed that I did not speak. Neither centered enough for an ordinary conversation nor prepared to explain why I had called her, I hung up.

Why did I get this message? Checking my inner dynamics at that time, I finally concluded that particular belief patterns that I had adopted in childhood but now outgrown were dying off and vanishing. That was a much more satisfactory answer! So began my process of examining inner messages and not necessarily taking what I heard at face value.

Simple Ways to Listen Inwardly

I cultivate inner listening by doing spiritual exercises plus journal writing about any inner awareness. Any consistent form of meditation could have a similar calming and centering effect, allowing you to be more aware of your inner dialogue. These practices can keep the inner connection clear.

Reflection and contemplation are also excellent ways to listen inwardly. Simply sit in silence, and give yourself time to be with yourself. Pay attention to the various thoughts and feelings bubbling around in your consciousness, or focus on some issue or uplifting quality. You could call this neutral loving observation of your inner awareness.

Intention for Inner Listening

Whether listening through spiritual exercises, meditation, reflection, or contemplation, you might find it helpful to start with an intention to clarify an issue. I like to write intentions in a journal prior to spiritual exercises and then jot down whatever answers come forward. For instance, I have written the following notes:

- For the highest good, I would like clarity and understanding on how to release my hurt feelings from yesterday's conversation.
- In the light for the highest good, I want guidance and direction on next steps with our upcoming presentation.
- I want light for clarity on how best to help my friend with this latest challenge!
- I want light for how best to talk to my boss about complications on the new project.
- I want to embrace whatever God wants me to know today for the highest and best.
- I want light for the highest good for my spiritual direction and inspiration.

Once you clarify your intention, you need not hold your thoughts to a single focus. Ideas could conform to logic, or they could float through the ether in helter-skelter fashion. If your mind wanders way off track, return to focus on the issue, and simply restate what you want to clarify. Many times, I do not get specific answers during a particular session of inner listening. I try not to demand but to remain open and receptive. Answers may come in another session, in a discussion with friends, or during an aha moment as I am walking the dogs.

Media moments—audios, videos, or articles—could trigger valuable new awareness, moving me closer to answers.

Clearing Space for Wisdom

Listening within creates a clear space for heart-centered wisdom to emerge. Usually I *hear* my own thoughts, but a wiser version of myself is speaking. Less often, with deepest gratitude, I hear the still, small voice of that which is divine, a voice that speaks far beyond my own wisdom. I recognize this voice as always loving, clear, and true.

Heart-Centered Wisdom

Being the NLO while you listen allows space for heart-centered wisdom to emerge. This wisdom could come as a clear vision, loving words, a special feeling, or a simple knowingness. When we follow wisdom from the heart's center, we lead ourselves forward in a kind of grace. We choose loving instead of judging. We accept what is, and peace fills body, mind, and spirit. We find answers. We take courage. We dare to take next gentle steps, creating the future we long for ... now.

Putting Pieces Together: Stress, Neutral Loving Observation, and Heart-Centered Wisdom

Remember how in chapter 5 I indicated that stress can be a wonderful teacher?

When a stressful situation arises, you recognize your usual symptoms—racing adrenaline or heartbeat, dry mouth, neck and shoulder tension, a knot in your stomach, and/ or a lump in your throat. These reactions are far from fun, but they are also clues to move to self-nurturing fast! They let you know that you do not like the situation, that you feel out of control or threatened, or that you have previously experienced similar harm, injury, or loss at some level.

In order to learn from this stressful situation, first move to the position of neutral loving observer. Silently declare a time out for your racing thoughts and feelings. Just listen within, or look inwardly at what is going on. Ask yourself, "What is really happening here?" Be willing to see yourself and others from a new perspective.

Breathe. Watch. Listen. Observe your inner reactions at least as much as the outer situation or other people who are involved. If you hear words, you might jot them down. If you turn within and see images, sketch them, or describe them in words.

What Is Happening Now?

In a stressful situation, I often say, "Hmmm. What's happening just now?" I might see that I am out of balance because of someone else's comment, because of his or her action, or perhaps because of the pressure I put on myself to hurry up and *get everything done now!*

Sometimes I observe that I am feeling stressed because I misunderstood or over-reacted, and then my frustration vanishes. I see more clearly, and I am emotionally okay after all! Stress melts away with clear understanding.

Other times I can recognize that frustrating people are merely doing their jobs. I see that I have choices in how to respond to their rules or their attitudes. I can be abrasive, or I can be kind but persistent and assertive in asking for what I need. Often, if I simply state my frustration with their system and ask for help in how to achieve my goal, doors open, and I can move forward.

When I feel stress with a seemingly immovable obstacle or when I have experienced harm or loss, being the neutral loving observer lets me assess the situation calmly. Being the NLO helps me accept that I need to cooperate with what is present now and perhaps research other options later.

To move to a level of learning from this stress, try asking yourself key questions. *What am I supposed to learn from this? How can I use this right now to learn and grow?*

Still being the neutral loving observer, listen and look inwardly for your heart-centered wisdom response. Perhaps your heart says simply, "Wait," or maybe it has another question to ask in the situation. Decide on your action steps and then take them.

Checklist for Letting Stress Be a Teacher

- Take a neutral loving observer time-out.
- Ask, "What is really happening here?"
- Observe your inner reactions.
- Be willing to see yourself and others in new ways.

- Ask, "What am I to learn from this? How can I use this to learn and grow?"
- Listen or watch for your heart-centered wisdom.
- Decide on your action steps and move forward with loving for yourself and all involved.

You are not blaming anyone else. You are taking responsibility for taming your stress through learning in the moment. You are accessing your own inner wisdom. Using your NLO, you are turning a stress-monkey into a valuable teacher.

What Did I Just Hear?

Journaling keeps your awareness grounded in our practical shared-reality world and supports neutral loving observation of your inner process.

Writing down your awareness in the moment helps you discern the difference between your ordinary, ego-centered awareness and your authentic inner wisdom. Are your perceptions being influenced by your own desires or fears?

Promptly capturing any significant awareness allows you to review it later for greater clarity and understanding. Read your words and imagine following through on the inner advice or developing that idea in some practical way. Does this fit your needs or provide inspiration for new direction?

A written record lets you reflect and check out inner impressions with practical steps forward. Do your tentative steps seem on track? Are you discovering enthusiasm or a sense of right action as you go? Have you been ignoring inner advice or cooperating with suggested directions? What are your results to date?

Practical Applications

As you gain confidence, you may well find that your inner wisdom has been working on your behalf all along. That little voice may speak quietly while you are working, talking, driving, or doing any simple task. Now you can be more consciously aware of it.

During a busy day, I often ask inwardly for clarity and understanding about next steps when it comes to a project or an issue that needs to be resolved. Then I take a moment to listen inwardly. If I am open and receptive, whatever comes up may lead to exactly the understanding I need. When an idea comes present, I like to scribble immediately in my "anything goes" notebook. Anchoring and preserving new awareness with a few written words captures action steps, enables reflection for clear understanding, and helps me observe my progress over time.

Sometimes the process is as simple as taking a deep breath, saying, "Okay, light. Now what?" And I will remember the thing that needs completing. Perhaps I need to get a birthday card for my brother and mail it now! If I cannot take action immediately, I jot down a reminder for later in the day.

Go Back to the University

Listening inwardly is fun as well as practical. Once in a triple-digit heat wave in Las Vegas, I drove a university car on business. After my first errand, I clearly heard a voice in my head say, "Go back to the university." I argued with that voice for a minute, but it was so insistent that I drove back to campus, planning to complete my business the next day. The next morning, not ten feet from my parking space, the same car sputtered out of gas. A phone call quickly brought a gas can to my rescue, and then I filled up at the campus pump. Thank goodness that I did not hit empty across town in yesterday's heat.

Yes, I *should* have been paying attention to the gas gauge, but since I didn't, wasn't it wonderful that an angel or a wiser part of me was looking out for me ... and that I listened?

Step-by-Step Guidelines for Inner Listening

- Set aside a few minutes in which you can be undisturbed to practice, or you can practice at the beginning of your meditation session.
- Ask for light for the highest good, or use your own prayer as you wish.
- Mentally clarify or write an intention or the question you hope to resolve.
- Take a minute or two to listen and a minute or two to jot down any words or ideas that arise in the quiet.

Clarifying Your Intention or Question

"Should I do X, Y, or Z?" calls for a yes or no answer. Instead, ask open-ended questions and look for greater understanding *so you can make a good decision consciously.* For instance, you can tell yourself the following:

- I'd like a new perspective on how to handle my big project.
- I'd like clarity and understanding on next steps in my relationship, especially regarding how to take better care of myself.
- I'm asking to be shown the most loving solutions that will work for me and all involved.
- Please help me see how to use this situation to learn and grow for the highest good.

Listening with Discernment

Engage your neutral loving observer. Whatever you hear inwardly, ask yourself, "Is the message loving?" Is it giving you positive, healthy, wise advice? Or is it reflecting your hopes, wishes, and desires, telling you what your ego wants to hear? Is it reflecting your fears, anger, and hurts? Pay attention. Judging yourself is not necessary. Simply observe. Take notes. Be the compassionate scientist observing yourself and listening.

Sometimes I used to receive messages with symbols that did not necessarily make sense with my practical life. Is your message a metaphor or full of symbols? You can do your best to decipher the symbols in terms of what they mean to you at this time. Or you can ask your inner awareness to provide messages in ways that you can easily understand and use! I have also learned that sometimes there simply is not an answer yet! I need to be patient.

Listening for Higher Understanding

A loving presence or feeling will accompany words of higher understanding. If the inner awareness is not loving, it is not from your higher self but some reflection from your ego or perhaps a fragment of cultural consciousness. My best guideline is this: Go with the love. If there is no love, hold, wait, and watch.

Capturing Your Awareness

Jot down relevant thoughts or a sense of knowing that arises either during the meditation or when you conclude an inner listening session. I find it easier to write things down in the moment, as they have a way of escaping consciousness when I go into deeper inner awareness.

A Note about Following Inner Wisdom

Over the years there have been times when I felt clear about some inner perception or decision, yet the situation did not turn out as happily as I expected or wished. There have also been times when I ignored that still, small voice within and did not like the results. In each case, I learned and grew significantly!

I learned that instead of bounding into action based on what seems like good inner guidance, I am well-served to take time to check out my plan, do my research, take a few tentative steps, and see what happens. Does this look as good as it sounded inwardly? I also learned to pay attention to that very quiet inner voice that holds great wisdom for me. I became more discerning about my emotions and about how my fears, desires, hopes, and expectations can color my inner wisdom.

Check messages with common sense. If an inner voice says, "Go jump in the lake!" in the middle of winter, look for symbolic meaning, or acknowledge your own inner conflict and learn from it. If you get this message at the beach when you are in your swimsuit, the water is safe, and you can swim, great! Jump right in, and have fun! If you should ever hear self-destructive messages, please seek help from your doctor or a qualified mental health professional. It is always your responsibility to check out the inner messages with common sense. You are accountable for your own actions and choices.

Wherever you are in your process, whatever is next for you spiritually, take those steps in loving and joy. Listen and learn well. Own the spiritual nature within you. That loving consciousness is who you really are for eternity.

CHAPTER 10

Meditation

The essence of spirituality is not found in books or sermons but in the quiet of the human heart.

Everyone is spiritual. Some are more consciously awake to their spiritual essence. I meet many people who express stirrings of their spiritual nature as a deep yearning for *something more* than everyday life experiences. After a lifetime of my own seeking and finding, I can only encourage each one who longs for that invisible *something more* to turn within.

Portals to Spiritual Experience

This chapter offers portals for opening and exploring your own spiritual experiences. If these simple practices appeal to you, see suggested readings at the end of this book, or turn to your own faith traditions for guidance on how to deepen your experience of inner awareness.

You may practice any religion or philosophy (or none of them at all), and you may be open to transcendent moments of spiritual peace, love, and joy. You simply need to turn within. If you need someone to show the way for next steps, you will find the one you need. Your guidance may appear as a person, a book, or even a movie or song that touches your heart deeply and helps you move forward and lift upward in consciousness.

I yearned for something more from an early age and attempted to turn within for answers. I began on my ninth birthday when I lay awake and asked myself, "Who am I?" That night, I concluded I was part of the world, the galaxy, the universe, and therefore also a part of God. As a young teen, I talked to God while ironing my dad's shirts, receiving plenty of good advice! As a teen, I observed my friends from strict churchgoing families with rules like no drinking, no smoking, or no dancing. Several sets of their parents divorced because one or both were smoking, drinking, or having affairs. I grew very disillusioned with churches! Yet I still had that longing for something more.

In my late twenties, thanks to a blind date, I discovered meditation. I gravitated to the practice like a flower to the sun. Peace? Relaxation? More energy? Spiritual? It couldn't hurt. I plunged in and never looked back.

As it turned out, meditating with a guru from India moved me from being agnostic to having a deep relationship with the Christ and God and a longing for even more. Meditating created a foundation for ongoing inner awareness and spiritual growth.

Many Forms of Meditation

My *Unabridged Random House Dictionary* says that to meditate is "to engage in thought or contemplation, reflect; to engage in transcendental meditation, devout religious contemplation, or quiescent spiritual introspection."

There are many forms of meditation—focusing on a mantra, practicing mindfulness, emptying the mind, moving, walking, visualizing, relaxing in nature or with music, contemplating, prayer and inner listening, and doing spiritual exercises. Since there are so many types of meditation, if the first one or two you try don't seem to fit, please explore other forms to find one that matches your faith, goals, needs, and lifestyle.

Why is meditation so popular now? It works on many levels, from simple stress reduction to profound spiritual awareness. Meditation slows breathing and brain waves, lowers blood pressure, relaxes muscles and organs, and decreases stress hormones, providing a reprieve from our usual rapid-fire mode of coping. It quiets the mind and allows expansion of consciousness. My many friends who meditate or do spiritual exercises seem calm on a daily basis even while active and enthusiastic. Meditators tend gradually to increase inner peace, clarity, intuition, and spirituality according to their faith.

Most any form of meditation done consistently can create a positive shift in consciousness. Meditation can help you live as a neutral loving observer, enjoy a stress-free sanctuary, or gain greater awareness of the presence of spirit. Whether you seek an island of calm in your day or deep spiritual awakening, meditation is a powerful form of self-nurturing.

Begin an adventure in self-discovery, or spark a love affair with God!

A Taste of Meditation

I want to give you a taste of meditation now. If you wish, you can incorporate this lovely practice into your nurturing routine. If you like it, there are many resources for further learning (see suggested readings.)

Meditation is not weird or elaborate. It is natural and simple. Are you sitting quietly as you read? To begin meditating is as simple as closing your eyes and becoming aware of your breath moving in and out. Try it. Close your eyelids, and take several natural, relaxed breaths in and out. Simply be aware of your breath and how it moves through your body.

You did it, right? You might have noticed that your face and jaw muscles relaxed or that your stomach moved more freely with each inhalation. You might have felt a moment of tranquility. If you are short of sleep, perhaps you felt ready to nod off.

Want to Know More?

Do a little more. Go for three to five minutes, and simply observe your breath. You might notice sounds in the room like the air conditioning, a door opening or closing, a clock ticking, or people talking outside. You may notice your own thoughts spiraling around as you focus on your breathing, or perhaps your to-do list is loudly updating itself! All of this is fine. You simply continue to focus on your breathing, gently observe these outer and inner experiences, and let them be. If you find yourself attending only to the outer distractions or you are focusing only on your thoughts, gently bring your awareness back to your breathing as many times as necessary.

Give it a try.

Okay, you just did a mini meditation. How do you feel? Compared with a few minutes earlier, what differences do you notice in your body? Are you warmer, cooler, or more relaxed? Is your pulse or breathing slower? Do you sense any differences in your mind or emotions? Are your thoughts slowing a bit? Are you feeling a little calmer? Do you notice any other changes? All of these are natural shifts. You may experience a few of them, or you may notice other natural changes as your mind, body, and emotions all settle into a more peaceful state.

One More Step?

For a traditional form of meditation, add a sacred sound, word, or phrase to help focus your mind as you remain aware of your breath. You simply repeat your word or words silently, attending to the sound as well as your breath. If you find you are distracted and no longer aware of your meditation process, gently bring your awareness back to your breath and your word(s).

A simple test for choosing a word or mantra is to try one for a few sessions. As you use one, do you feel uplifted, peaceful, and loving? If you feel jangled, disturbed, or subtly out of sorts, that form may not be a match for you. Some other type might work very well. Here are a few classics that I have enjoyed.

- Peace. Simply repeat the word "peace."
- *Om* or *aum.* This famous mantra is pronounced like home without the h. It is Sanskrit for all of creation.
- *Shanti.* Pronounced shahn-tee, this is Sanskrit for peace.
- *Ananda.* Pronounced ah-nahn-dah, *Ananda* is Sanskrit for love.
- *Christos Ananda.* Pronounce *Christos* as a Spanish word, or like the proper name Chris plus toast without the final t. It translates as the Christ of love.
- One. This is a generic, non-spiritual focus word from Herbert Benson's book, *The Relaxation Response.*
- *Ani-Hu.* Prounounced ah-nigh hugh, this translates from Sanskrit as empathy or compassion with God. I have included specific instructions for how to do spiritual exercises using the Ani-Hu, at the end of this book.

What uplifting words or phrases would you add? What could become a sacred or centering focus for you? Here are some possibilities: *Love. Light. I am. I am peace. I am love. God and I are one. Living in loving. Sanctify me. God's will be done.* Experiment with a few that appeal to you. Are there special words from your faith tradition that lend themselves to meditation? Try the name of your faith leader, such as Jesus or Buddha.

However you approach meditation, one gigantic benefit of regular practice is that you become more attuned to your authentic self, your soul, which is connected to God and to the divine essence in each living being. In addition to providing relaxation, meditation or spiritual exercises can deeply nurture your spiritual self.

CHAPTER 11

Nurturing a Positive Focus

Negative thoughts may show up.
Do not resist them, but keep returning your
attention to positive focus on your goal instead.

I Think I Can

My adventure with nurturing positive focus started on a Saturday morning when I was six. My younger brother and sister were elsewhere with Dad. I could hear Mother clinking a bowl and spoon, stirring up cupcakes. The scent of lilacs wafted on balmy air through the screen door. Robins and sparrows squabbled over choice tidbits in our front yard. I stretched comfortably on my belly, my cheek pressed to a large pink rose in the living room carpet. I could smell faintly the dust stirred up by Mama's vigorous vacuuming.

From the big brown Motorola on a shelf by the picture window came my favorite program, *Big John and Sparky.* I listened with all my might as Big John's rich, deep voice washed over me, bringing to life Watty Piper's story of *The Little Engine That*

Could. When the full-size locomotives were out of commission, the Little Engine got a huge job. Chug, chug. *I think I can. I think I can.* Puff, puff. *I think I can. I think I can.* He pulled that big train all the way to the top of the mountain! He did it!

As Big John triumphantly concluded the story, electrical energy charged through my body. I leapt from the carpet and shot out the front door, bursting with my secret, silently chanting, "I think I can. I think I can!" I exploded with enthusiasm. Joy and amazement sizzled in me. I paced around my front yard, letting this remarkable tool settle into my heart!

Big John transformed my life that morning. *I think I can. I think I can!* I put this little saying to work like a mantra. Naturally rather quiet, bookish, and timid around strangers, when I faced a new challenge or felt anxious about a new task, I rolled out my magic words. *I think I can.* I learned to introduce myself to grown-ups with a handshake and to ride a bike. I became the only girl on the block who could ride no hands, no feet. I read a pamphlet on how to water ski and got up successfully on my first try. Playing school on the front porch, I taught a dozen younger neighbors the power of the mantra, *I think I can!*

Reading and Practicing

I discovered more about positive thinking in my elementary years, reading Mom's *Ladies' Home Journal*. Because of my "I think I can" focus, I not only read but also practiced tips like how to be a better friend by listening carefully, thinking kind thoughts, and expecting the best from the other person. In junior high I discovered Norman Vincent Peale and Dale

Carnegie on library shelves. I added their positive thinking wisdom to my heart.

In my early thirties, in addition to meditating daily, I explored with Ernest Holmes, James and Myrtle Fillmore, Emmet Fox, Florence Scovell Schinn, Eric Butterworth, Louise Hay, Shakti Gawain, and many more who demonstrated the art of positive thinking, affirmations, and visualizations. I devoured *A Course in Miracles (ACIM)*. For about five years, I worked these lessons daily and wrote my professional paper for my first master's degree comparing the rational-emotive therapy of psychologist Albert Ellis with *A Course in Miracles.* Using positive words and images became a way of life and a powerful tool for personal growth and problem solving.

Positive Focus

What's the point of being positive? Plenty of old sayings embody practical truths. Like attracts like. What you give out you get back. What goes around comes around. Turn lemons into lemonade. Look on the bright side. Every cloud has a silver lining.

If people more easily focus in this direction, we peg them as optimists. Research indicates that optimists are happier, healthier, and more successful. On the other hand, people who naturally lean toward pessimism often do well in life because they consider and avoid potential problems. Many of us simply bounce from positive to negative at the mercy of circumstance and mood.

Some philosophies maintain that you need to hold positive thoughts all the time or risk attracting negative experiences. I prefer the idea of positive focus as presented by John-Roger in an interview by Allan Richards in *New Millennium*, October/ November 1998.

> A positive thought can be eliminated by a negative thought. In fact, it takes 25 positive thoughts to erase a negative thought. A positive focus cannot be eliminated. It is a direction and allows for negativity, falling, and setbacks. It is an intention that we persist in regardless of the conditions we encounter. A Spiritual Warrior would view it this way, "He wins who endures to the end."

I am not failing if I temporarily host a negative thought! I can use any negative ideas or experiences as references for learning, set myself up to avoid problems, and simply return to my positive focus over and over. Because negative stuff creeps in with so many news bytes, conversations, and daily hassles, I do mean *again and again ... and again!*

My suggestion is that when you pick up negative snippets from the media or other people, react with knee-jerk negativity to people close to you, or simply indulge in "poor me" thinking, do not judge these slips into negativity. Simply acknowledge any challenge, pain, or issue, so you can overcome it.

Be willing to examine a challenge in practical, realistic terms—from worst to best case—and to consider a variety of solutions. This is a little like focusing in meditation or being the neutral loving observer. Negative thoughts may show up. Do not resist them, but keep returning your attention to positive focus on your goal instead.

When you simply observe options and return to a positive focus as quickly as possible, you will find that over time, the positive far outweighs the negative. Your predominating habit of positive focus helps you stay balanced and on purpose.

Holding a positive focus is a giant key for self-nurturing. You set yourself up for success by consistently returning to the positive despite any doubts or setbacks. With a verbal and visual template (see chapter 16) of what you want, you move forward with purpose and direction, creating win-win solutions. Rather than waiting for life to deliver random events, you create your own reality. Your positive thoughts trigger positive emotions. You feel better, act better, look better, and do better. You trust yourself and make better choices. Confidence grows. You become more spontaneous and creative. Your spacious consciousness embraces new ideas and adventures. You create an inner climate of thriving.

Active Loving Intention: Your Ally in Positive Focus

Active loving intention (or taking action on your intention with love) is your ally in bringing your heart's desires to life. Once you identify what you want and intend to realize for the highest good, you lovingly demonstrate your intention by becoming active. If you want to play guitar, you call the friend who promised to teach you to strum chords and unearth the instrument from your closet. For a new career, you put your resume on search engines, actively seek out companies of interest, and network with friends and social media connections. To develop confidence, you take a small risk or create one daring mini adventure each day! You nurture new directions with consistent small steps, following where active loving intention guides. Repeated tiny steps lead surely to your goal.

Part 4

Fine-Tuning Change: More Gentle Strategies

Chapters 12 to 20 offer strategies for self-nurturing to add as you wish to your basic program. Use these as suggested, or as reference points to similar practices that you already know work well for you.

CHAPTER 12

Nurturing Your Future Now: Naming Your Heart's Desires

*With written heart's desires, you are
far more likely to succeed.*

This is a straightforward exercise in identifying your heart's desires so that you know where you want to go in this journey called life. You might complete it in one evening, or you might use several smaller chunks of time, adding to your list periodically and then consolidating to identify your truest directions and goals. I now tend to revisit my list about once a year and update it, but when I began, I tweaked it more often.

A Starting Point: What Do You Want?

To hold a positive focus, it is useful to identify your direction, wants, goals, or intentions (i.e., your heart's desires). When you cut through the fluff, what do you truly want physically, emotionally, mentally, and spiritually? What do you want in your health, relationships, family, career, finances, home, recreation, education, and creative expression?

I suggest that you pause right now and make notes of what you most desire to create or enhance in your life experience. Try to keep in mind that what you list is for the highest good of you and all concerned. Write in your journal, make notes in your digital device, or scratch on a napkin. Capture your thoughts in writing. With written desires, you are far more likely to succeed.

Brainstorm. Look at the levels of consciousness (physical, emotional, mental, spiritual) and major areas of your life, such as relationships (including the one with yourself), career, finances, health, exercise, nutrition, learning and education, sexuality, creativity, recreation and fun, and so on. Be specific. To start this process, list anything from new socks to a new career, a wonderful relationship, or grand enlightenment!

If your wish list includes specific issues you want to release, like excessive anger or anxiety, flip them to the positive equivalent. For instance, if you wish to release anxiety to experience inner peace, inner peace should go on your list. To release asthma and allergies, you might aim for breathing fully, freely, and easily.

Heart's Desires

After creating a thorough want list, aim to condense and consolidate so that the ten to fifteen *most important* items emerge. These are the major desires of your heart, a starting point for your practice of positive focus. With your master list, you can nurture yourself with numerous strategies, such as positive focus, active loving intention, affirmations or positive self-talk, and verbal or visual self-nurturing templates.

CHAPTER 13

Upgrade Your Story

*If you create a new explanation, a positive, upbeat story
of how you overcame obstacles and made decisions
that turned out to support you, perhaps in unexpected
ways, you will be nurturing a new mind-set every time
you explain your personality or circumstances.*

What Is Your Story?

What story do you tell yourself and others to explain how
you happen to be the way you are? Your story is what you
tell yourself about why your life is the way it is. It is really
answering your own big *why* questions. Your story explains
and defines yourself to yourself and by extension, to others.
Your story can be your whole life story or simply the latest
drama in your life. Either is a good place to start with
transformation.

When you repeatedly tell a story of being put down, victimized,
limited, or stuck, you have lots of room for nurturing
and transformation! If you create a new explanation, a

positive, upbeat story of how you overcame obstacles and made decisions that turned out to support you perhaps in unexpected ways, you will be nurturing a new mind-set every time you explain your personality or circumstances.

If someone has suggested that you "change your story" but you wonder how to go about it, here are some approaches I have used. They will help you tease out the components of your story and transform them. As a self-nurturing practice, you can change one element of your story at a time. In a year, you will experience a much lighter, brighter life.

I Am Willing to See This Differently

One of the most helpful approaches for changing my story came to me from Louise Hay. I believe I heard this advice on one of her audio products about twenty-five years ago and have been using it ever since! I learned I could simply say, "I am willing to see this differently."

If you are having difficulty reframing an element of your past or present story and turning a problem into a challenge or if you feel stuck, victimized, powerless, confused, unsure, angry, and/ or frustrated, repeat this affirmation a few times. Say it every time you find that negative state popping up and watch what happens in your consciousness over the next few hours or days.

Reframe a Problem into a Challenge

Your story no doubt chronicles many obstacles or problems that you encountered.

Years ago I took to heart an idea from the movie *Up the Down Staircase*. If something seems like an obstacle, see it as a challenge instead. Almost automatically now when people discuss a problem or an issue, I like to clarify the challenge. For instance, I may say, "Our challenge is how to create a more effective marketing program for millennials." Or I may say to myself, "My current challenge is completing this book with excellence and authenticity."

In your current life, check out the power of language by considering your problems as challenges. When you shift a problem into a challenge, you imply that you are up for the process and expect to succeed. The next time you face an obstacle, remember you are simply facing your next steps to success. Rather than feeling stymied, focus on the challenge and expand your feeling of empowerment and adventure.

In examining your personal story, you might observe places where you tend to say, "The problem is— If only they had not done— If only I had been more—" These are potential touchstones for transformation. Change the wording of your story to reflect the challenge. Now you can say, "The challenge for me at that time was— Since they did not do something, my challenge became overcoming— Since I was not more of something, I took on the challenge to become—"

Claim the Learning

One powerful way to upgrade your story is to focus on what you learned from the situation, painful though it may have been. You can say, "There were many challenges then, but I am extracting the learning and moving forward in balance and harmony." As a more specific example, you might say, "Because of the hurricane, I learned that people are more important than things and that I am an amazing survivor!"

It might help to list specific things you learned from a traumatic event. How did you grow? What unexpected benefits emerged from the situation? Did you strengthen yourself, or gain more compassion for others? Maybe you did not see these positive outcomes for many years, but you begin to see them now.

Complete Incompletes

Other clues for transforming your story might show up in emotions and judgments that leak out at certain spots in your narrative. These emotions or judgments indicate you have unfinished business to complete at that point to free your energy and move on. Forgive the self-judgments. Observe your emotions and underlying beliefs about problems. Take any action steps needed, such as tossing photos of a former lover. Lovingly declare the situation complete. Let it go, and move forward.

Getting rid of unfinished craft projects, unfiled papers, and unread books could lift a weight as heavy as any emotional drag on your story and your energy. Think about those clothes that you have saved for ten years just in case your weight changes again. These are symbolic, unconscious elements of your story that are hiding in plain sight. The more you can complete, clear out, or clear up, the easier it gets to tell a new story.

Your story is a reflection of an evolving self. When you focus on your learning, completing unfinished business, and overcoming challenges, it becomes triumphant.

CHAPTER 14

Affirmations to Anchor Intentions

*You create new pathways in consciousness
to create a new reality.*

Affirmations

Ever since grade school and especially since the late 1970s, I have used positive thoughts and affirmations extensively. Positive thoughts and self-talk lead to happier, more loving moods and much more successful outcomes. Affirmations are positive statements that you generally repeat many times to help create positive outcomes or manifest your heart's desires.

Many books focus on affirmations and include useful statements that might fit your needs. When I was new to this work, I found a few authors particularly helpful—Louise Hay, Catherine Ponder, Florence Scovell-Schinn, and John-Roger. Please see the suggested reading list at the end of this book. Check with your preferred bookseller or library, and remember that you can request books through interlibrary loan if your library does not have a particular text.

The beauty of working with affirmations is that over time you may learn to use positive language for just about everything. Awareness of positive word choices can make it easier and easier to maintain a positive focus. Your affirmations will naturally be a form of self-nurturing, and they will help to bring forward chosen qualities and create or attract more positive experiences and relationships.

Words that Ring True

Affirmations are verbal building blocks to let your consciousness know your new direction. You are giving instructions to both your conscious and unconscious mind. The unconscious mind operates in the present tense. Everything is immediate, so state an affirmation in the present tense as if it is happening right now. Take your time to create your affirmations. Test them until they look, sound, and feel right for you. Say the words that ring true in your heart, and then allow your multidimensional self to cooperate in bringing forward your heart's desires.

Some people resist affirmations because they feel as though speaking them is like lying to themselves. Please do not get hung up on feeling that you are lying to yourself if you make positive statements about something that is not yet present physically in your life. You are creating new pathways in consciousness in order to generate a new reality.

A Great Way to Begin

If you want to create your own affirmations, imagine the outcome you are aiming for, and make a positive statement describing it, intending your action for the highest good. Start with "I am." Add an action verb ending in "-ing." Add your positive outcome.

I am nurturing myself into transformation.

Add some adjectives, adverbs, or a simple clause to make it uniquely yours. Consider the following: *Every day I am caring for myself exquisitely! I am easily and naturally holding in my inner peace. I am loving myself just as I am, enjoying my adventure of learning and growing.*

As with listing your heart's desires, keep your outcome positive. For instance, avoid saying, "I am not smoking," or, "I will not get angry." Instead you can say the following: *I am happily smoke-free. I am happy as a nonsmoker. I am holding in my calm and peace. Regardless of challenges around me, I am at peace.*

Famous Last Words

Modern psychology supports this long-established practice for creating affirmations. Memory research indicates that we easily remember and mentally focus on the last few words we hear. In psychology classes I would demonstrate this by telling students, "For the next few minutes, do not think about polka-dotted elephants. No! Whatever you do, please, no thinking about polka-dotted elephants. You will lose points on your next test if you think about polka-dotted elephants!"

A quick check with the smirking class revealed that of course, they were all thinking about spotted elephants!

So nurture yourself with last words that are clearly positive reflections of what you truly want. *Today, I am joyfully successful! I am happily completing my excellent term paper now!*

Sensory Reinforcement

Because using multiple senses helps to anchor learning, I often start by speaking affirmations aloud while walking, or I write, speak, and then read them once daily. Silently repeating affirmations engages your mind. Speaking them, you naturally also hear yourself. Reading engages your visual sense. Walking, or writing positive statements by hand, brings in your kinesthetic (feeling or touch) senses. Using any combination of sensory inputs helps to reinforce your affirmations. In general, whatever the goal you wish to manifest, you want to see yourself being, doing, and having it. The words help you to imagine it, and having a picture of yourself enjoying what you truly want enables you to find words to describe it.

If you can add rhythm, rhyme, or melody and recite or sing an affirmation, that's even better. Here is one of my rhymes.

> I choose to be on time.
> I finish what I start.
> I share my words with care,

> Discerning from my heart.
> My feelings are my own,
> I change them with my mind.
> I take next steps with ease
> And leave the past behind.

The next one is an old favorite. As I drove around Las Vegas in the 1980s, I made this up and sang it to myself a few thousand times, and I revive it occasionally today. For my simple tune, check my website, www.IlenyaMarrin.com.

> I love myself.
> I accept myself.
> I'm my own
> Very, very, very best friend.

Affirming for Another

If you want to affirm for the good of someone else, I strongly suggest that you include the "for the highest good" clause so that you are not inadvertently manipulating the other person. Although we might think we know best, we do not necessarily truly know what another person needs. As painful as it might be for me to watch someone struggling with challenges, from a higher spiritual perspective, that person may be having his or her perfect experience. The individual may be learning exactly what he or she needs to learn. My friend's shoulder injury may be helping her learn to be more watchful in daily activities, to slow down and reflect on her life, or to allow family members to assist her for a change.

Because I do not want to unconsciously manipulate my friend, I would say, "For the highest good (or in the light for the highest good), Corey is now enjoying perfect health." Or I might say, "Light for the highest good for healing for Corey's shoulder."

CHAPTER 15

Nurturing Positive Focus through Language

Transforming your language honors yourself, helps you maintain positive focus in the moment, and nurtures you by preserving your personal space and time.

Do you remember that I said affirmations could help you begin to use positive language more often?

Now I am inviting you to be more aware of language. Are there specific words that leave you feeling disempowered, stuck, anxious, or fearful? If so, consciously substitute more empowering words and phrases at every opportunity. Experiment. Microscopic steps will add up to major progress. With more positive words, your emotions might settle, and your sense of self-worth could blossom. You may enjoy more confidence, love, and inner peace. Practice, practice, practice.

Transforming your language honors yourself, helps you maintain positive focus in the moment, and nurtures you by preserving your personal space and time. It does not make you mean or unsociable but more authentic.

Noticing habitual negative language patterns is a first step. Here are a few of my favorite ways to nurture positive focus through language. These basics will boost your awareness of word choices and jump-start your process of transformation. Be the neutral loving observer, and do not judge yourself. Simply note negative word choices and experiment with substituting positive or neutral words. Observe and learn from the results.

Should, must, ought to

No *shoulding* on yourself! Should and its buddies imply an attitude of resistance and a judgment. Instead, experiment with saying, "I could if I wanted to." For example, you could say the following:

- *I really should mow the lawn this afternoon since rain is predicted for tomorrow.* Here's what's implied: "I don't really want to, but if I don't, I'm not being responsible." This is a subtle self-judgment. Forgive yourself!
- *If I wanted to, I could mow the lawn this afternoon and be ahead of the rain tomorrow.* Here's what's implied: "I have a choice to cooperate with the weather, mow today, and be on top of my chores."
- *I don't really want to mow the lawn today, but if I do, I will be happy that I did because tomorrow's rain will make it grow tall and wild.* Here's what's implied: "I weigh my options. Will mowing today feel better than time spent on other activities, or is tall grass and a

messy cut in two days a good trade-off for spending time on other priorities?"

Observe your own subtle *should* moments. Experiment with saying instead, "I could, if I wanted to." When you change the wording, how do you feel? Are decisions easier? Do you move more quickly out of resistance and into either doing or not doing?

Too

What happens when you drop the comparative word *too*? Work to build a comfort level with simple neutral observations. "I am short." "Yes, she seems angry." Or choose descriptive words such as *notable, remarkable, very,* or *quite.* "That was a notable outburst of anger." No comparisons, no judgments, no dragging energy. Your language is now clear and straightforward.

I can't

Instead of saying, "I can't," which implies you are not able, try saying, "I don't want to right now." I mean it! Experiment.

The first few times I said those words, I waited for a thunderbolt from heaven. Hmmm. Nothing! Rather than being negative, saying, "I don't want to," is simply being accurate and self-empowering. You acknowledge your preference and honor yourself. If you are uncomfortable saying aloud, "I don't want to," at least acknowledge it to yourself. Inner honesty propels your self-nurturing success.

If you are saying, "I can't," to a heartfelt dream, switch your words by saying, "I don't want to." This time, observe and journal about any emotions, fears, or negative fantasies that come up. Writing will yield new understanding and impetus for change.

A friend once said, "I can't go back to school at fifty-four!" When she finally substituted "I don't want to" for her original phrase, a barrage of *reasons* flooded her mind. "I'm too old. I don't know how to study anymore. I can't keep up with younger students. I never was good at writing papers. It will be too expensive." Specific fears paraded before her mind's eye. In a few days, she researched and challenged each fear. She decided she *wanted* to attend graduate school, and she completed her master's degree just after her fifty-seventh birthday.

Notice whether you say, "I can't," when you feel trapped socially. Alternatively, do you want to please or win approval and say yes when you would rather say no? It's true confession time. My husband says I do "Texas make nice." I don't care what we call it. I prefer caring to abrasive approaches. My strategy is to have fun nurturing and being true to myself *and* kind to others. You may need to give yourself permission to say no in order to take care of yourself first. You can easily develop *gracious* ways to decline.

For straightforward situations, experiment with replies. *That won't work for me right now. No, I won't be with you that night. No thanks. That is not my cup of tea. I'm not the best person for that kind of job. I think you want someone who can— No, I'll be busy then.* (It is absolutely fine if *busy* means you will be reading a detective story at home.)

If you are not sure what you want to do, try saying, "Let me think about it (or meditate on it) and get back to you. I might, but I'm not sure yet. I could let you know by Tuesday." Take a few minutes to check in with your inner self, come to a clear decision, and let the person know. Whether you accept or decline, you can learn and grow from your choice and the results.

CHAPTER 16

Self-Nurturing Templates

Creating your own written or visual template for your heart's desires or a self-nurturing lifestyle can help maintain your positive focus.

A template is a pattern or mold that serves as a guide in a construction process. You are by now most likely somewhat involved in constructing a self-nurturing lifestyle. Creating your own verbal or visual template can help maintain your positive focus. I use both.

Written Self-Nurturing Template

To create your first written template, turn your list of heart's desires into a series of affirmations. Once you polish the template to your satisfaction, you might print a nice copy and read it once a day for many weeks, or you may record it and listen to it on your commute or at bedtime. I recorded my early versions over a favorite piece of instrumental music and listened faithfully on Los Angeles freeways to and from work.

Now I use a two-page template and read it most days either in the early morning or before bedtime. Every few months I update it and print a new version.

A simple way to organize a verbal self-nurturing template is to reflect on your list of desires and write at least one affirmation that captures what you want for each area. You may certainly write more as needed to clarify and fill out. You are aiming for positive statements that paint a picture in words or help you get a feeling of success and completion about each desire.

I always include at the top of my template, "In the light for the highest good."

As a suggestion, simply read your template once a day. You need not feel any urgency or passion with this reading. It is just to remind you of your positive focus. You might want to make a note in your journal whenever you find qualities from your self-nurturing template coming to fruition.

I used a form of a verbal template to manifest my relationship with my husband. While I was at the University of Santa Monica, I learned that it is important to claim as your own the qualities you seek in your mate when you are aiming to manifest a relationship. I had a long list of qualities that I wanted in a mate, and I made sure each one read, "I am and he is—"

Based on a classroom suggestion, I chose the quality I considered most important for myself. *I am and he is one hundred percent true to me.* I read this template each evening, and I focused on being true to myself throughout my daily activities. I sometimes asked myself what a mate that was true to me might do for me, and then I would give that to myself. For instance, I bought myself beautiful flowers a few times. How lovely! I took myself to lunch in nice restaurants. Fun! I said no to social events that felt like "make nice" obligations. Relief! Within about three months, I met the man I married. In him, I found all the qualities I had requested and more, and I have continued to develop those qualities in myself.

Visual Self-Nurturing Template: Visions that Shine

If you are strongly attuned to your visual sense, try creating a visual template or collage of images and words to capture a vision of your heart's desires. Collect old magazines with lots of pictures. My doctor's office is happy to give me an armload from the overflow in their waiting room if I ask a week or so in advance. You could include favorite greeting cards, stickers, photos, and pictures you might print from the Internet. If you do not find specific words you want, hand write or print them out. Spend a couple of hours paging through your collection and clipping any pictures or headline words that relate to your desires. Go quickly, and be intuitive. Include any images that speak to you. Make your collection fun, beautiful, and uplifting.

Get a poster board, a large sheet of construction paper, a canvas board, or other sturdy backing material. Spend another hour or more laying out your pictures and words in a way that is attractive and meaningful to you. Tape or glue them to the backing, and hang the collage where you will see it often, preferably in a protected place where others will not make fun of it or you.

As an alternative, draw or paint your vision. While chatting with classmates over dinner, a friend once sketched on a napkin her vision of her dream home. A year later, driving through a new neighborhood, she saw it with a "for sale" sign out front. Although she had not been thinking of buying, she contacted a realtor and learned she could indeed purchase the home. She turned it into a lovely, unique sanctuary that nurtured her and her pets for several years.

About ten years ago, I used colored pens to draw simple geometric forms and symbols and filled in with words describing my sacred desires. I framed the page and hung it in my bedroom, where I saw it casually every day. I still smile and feel a flood of warmth and loving whenever I look at it. In this case, my desires, which mostly involved inner qualities, have manifested beautifully.

I recently made a new collage with pictures and words I have been saving for some time. Reflecting my current active loving intentions and my desires, this colorful collection of images hangs over my desk and seems to infuse my office with enthusiasm and joy for my spiritual inspiration and creative work.

Nurture your current and future self by glancing at your template in passing, or spend a few moments reflecting on it each day. Seeing a vivid picture of your positive outcome triggers your powerful visual imagination. Pay attention, and see how your process of manifestation unfolds.

If you have children, this is a wonderful project to teach them how to manifest their own hearts' desires.

CHAPTER 17

Emotion: Ego Energy in Motion

*Your feelings, moods, or ee-motions are ego energy
moving around in your consciousness, providing
feedback about what is or is not working.*

Nurturing Your Emotional Level

Your emotional level of consciousness is connected to body,
mind, and spirit. When your emotions are balanced, you
naturally take good care of your physical self and feel more
able to handle your responsibilities with ease and grace.
Communication and relationships with others flow more
smoothly. When you feel calm, centered, and loving, you are
more open to spiritual inner awareness.

Emotional well-being relates very closely to positive
focus because your thoughts in large measure drive your
emotions, and emotional experiences influence thinking.
If you sincerely explore the strategies I share here and do
not find some positive results, or if you are dealing with
persistent or severe depression, anxiety, or other disorders,

please seek the help of a physician or qualified mental health professional. These self-nurturing strategies could be very helpful along with counseling or other treatment options.

Ego Energy in Motion

One fun and convenient way to look at emotions is to think of ego energy in motion or ee-motion. Your feelings, moods, or ee-motions are ego energy moving around in your consciousness, providing feedback about what is or is not working. These emotions are a part of your ego/personality structure. At times they appear to pop up unexpectedly, even randomly, but emotions typically occur as a response to conscious or subconscious thoughts, perceptions, or perhaps brain chemistry reactions to environmental signals. Sometimes your ee-motions move gently and quietly, other times dramatically. Ego energy in motion can tell you, "This is great. I am in bliss," or it can say, "I feel rotten, sad, betrayed, angry, abandoned, rejected, hurt, frustrated, and tense."

Many of us work diligently to avoid painful emotions. Frightened of our own moods, suspecting something might be dreadfully wrong, feeling miserably uncertain and out of control, we may try to cover and avoid negative emotions at a high cost. This approach doesn't work very well. Denying painful feelings and ignoring whatever problems triggered them may promote worse disturbances as our consciousness works overtime to keep unruly ee-motions under control. When we numb out the negative, we can also lose the ability to feel positive emotions.

All Emotions Are Useful

Hard-won experience has taught me to view emotions more positively. We don't need to fear dramatic emotions. We naturally prefer upbeat feelings, but all emotions are useful! They alert us to the need for different choices and behaviors when things are not working well, and they encourage us to repeat positive choices when life hums joyfully. As part of self-nurturing, we can learn from all our emotions, release or transform the triggers for negative emotions, and spend more time enjoying positive emotions by choice.

Observe Your Ee-motions

Regardless of how you feel, your core self is not broken. Your ego might be hurting; however, your essence as a living being is intact, and you can learn from the experience. For most of us, negative emotions are miserable, but denying or trying to ignore hurt can create subconscious icebergs of pain that will shake your whole system if something bumps them underwater. Trying to stuff down and put the lid on anger can be like putting a cap on a volcano. Who knows when it will blow? My work in counseling and social work confirms that while you don't want to be out of control emotionally, you don't need to stop, block, shut down, or deny emotions. Instead you can observe and accept your feelings, moods, and kinesthetic sensations *as indicators of what does and does not work for you.* Acknowledge when things feel out of balance, and become a detective to learn what triggered the off-kilter feelings. Make new choices to correct that triggering situation. Love yourself in the midst of your upset feeling.

When Ee-motions Erupt

Next time you feel those ee-motions moving, shift to being a neutral loving observer.

Watch your inner process. Listen to your self-talk—all sides of it! Pretend you are a curious and caring scientist studying this human being without interfering. From your neutral loving observer stance, view your upset self with compassion. Look for patterns, causes, reasons for the causes, and consequences of this particular line of ego energy in motion. As you observe, be aware of your breathing. Be with yourself in a neutral and supportive way. You are not trying to change anything. Simply observe. When you have a chance, make some journal notes on your experience. As the NLO, what did you learn by observing this round of ego energy in motion?

If you have difficulty stepping out of the emotions and into your neutral loving observer mode, it might help to imagine yourself standing at the top of a tall building or a mountain or hovering in a helicopter, looking down on the scene that triggered your ee-motions. What happened? Who was doing or saying what? How did you respond? From this higher level, be the neutral loving observer of any patterns involved in your process.

Transform Your Ee-motions

Wearing that "neutral loving observer" hat, consider what you could do differently in order to feel more balanced in this scenario. Are there things you do or words you think that consistently throw you into an emotional outburst? Do you react a certain way to a specific person or situation? Write a new screenplay for these situations. Just as you may have reframed situations from the past, reframe your future. Imagine a successful outcome for all involved, a wonderful win-win situation. This means an outcome in which *you* feel loving, centered, peaceful, satisfied, or content and in which others also feel successful. You do not have to know all the details about how you would achieve the successful outcome. Let that be. Simply imagine the emotional success as vividly as possible. Breathe into it. Be with it. Trust that such a state is possible.

If you find yourself stewing over this incident or worrying about similar problems in the future, vividly recall your neutral loving observation and envision the win-win outcome. You are taking small steps into new awareness and embracing new emotions simply by observing your inner process. Next time a similar situation pops up, do the best you can, and once more observe your inner process. Train yourself so that any time you start to feel emotional, you shift to being that neutral loving observer and notice what is happening from a higher, broader perspective.

From the NLO position overlooking your emotions, remember that you are not responsible for and can never change another person's behavior. You can nurture new responses to their behavior. Your observation gives you keys. Be open to new ideas and new action steps when such a situation arises again. As always, next steps are your choice.

You Are Bigger than Your Ee-motions

Yes, you may continue to feel uncomfortable energy in motion at times. So what? You are so much more than that particular energy. There may be a deep hurt from past traumatic experiences. That hurt ee-motion is a strong reminder of what doesn't work. What you do with past hurtful experiences is up to you. You might use them as valuable learning experiences and reference points as you make new, more workable choices.

And you might quit trying to get rid of uncomfortable energy in motion. Observe it. Use it to inform yourself. Look, listen, and sense. Feel that feeling in motion. Recognize it as part of the package you have assembled so far. Use it as an opportunity to learn and grow.

This feeling is not you. You are observing. Therefore, you are much bigger than that feeling.

Nurturing Choices with Ee-motions

You, the observer, have many choices. Experiment with any of these ideas. You can always use your own words along similar lines if you wish.

You could plunge right back into ee-motion and let that be your reality, forget about observing and self-nurturing, and indulge in painful drama until you got tired of doing that. Or you could choose to hold in your neutral loving observer and look at other choices.

You might simply choose to love and nurture yourself. You can ask yourself, "What's the most nurturing thing I can do for myself right now? What would help me relax into my true self in this situation? What would help me to remember who I am and to act from that center?"

Maybe the most nurturing thing is to take some action to solve a practical problem. Maybe you get a specific self-care idea when you go on a walk, take a nap or turn on uplifting music.

Or maybe you just breathe. Feel that calming presence of your breath. Lovingly observe. It's quieter and more peaceful. Maybe it has a humming quality … or a gentle rhythm like waves washing in on the shore. Get comfortable with this level beyond mere emotions. From inside your breath, observe your ee-motion. Breathe into your feeling. Let it be. There's no need to change anything. Just be in the moment. Be present, and observe the emotion. Keep breathing into it. Observe.

Often, simply breathing and observing your ee-motion for two or three minutes will bring a shift to a more neutral state or even to a loving and joyful state. I suggest you practice with small emotions like the frustration of standing in a long line when you are in a hurry, and gently expand your practice to include larger and more complex emotions as they arise.

I'm Loving This!

How about loving the situation even if it looks like a mess? *I'm loving this mess!* Adapted slightly from a suggestion to say "I love this,"[4] which is offered in the book *Momentum: Letting Love Lead* by John-Roger and Paul Kaye, this is one of my favorite quick adjustments when my ee-motions are unruly! Experiment.

I catch the beginnings of irritation, anxiety, or hurt feelings and tell myself, "I'm loving this."

I might be saying it through gritted teeth at first! But usually four or five repetitions have me laughing at the incongruity of loving this upsetting situation, and then I am free to choose my next steps from a place of balance. In that chuckle I am occupying my larger, wiser self (or my neutral loving observer), grasping the bigger picture. Here I am, a soul having a human experience, and this is another opportunity to observe, learn, nurture myself, and grow on many levels.

Accepting what is present emotionally allows for awareness and changes.

A quiet but adventurous friend has a slightly more active way of observing and accepting her ee-motions. Her favorite way to nurture herself out of a low mood is to allow herself to cry, to experience her thoughts and feelings of the moment, and to "listen to what comes out in the process." She writes out her feelings with angry, hard scribbles if necessary. Then she tears up and trashes or burns the pages. She often starts by writing, "What's going on here?" Then she lets the words flow and does not judge what she writes. When she throws her pages away, it is like taking out the garbage. She is lighter, brighter, and centered again.

John-Roger's Nine Magic Words

Here is one more strategy for settling ee-motions. In conflicts or tense, awkward social situations, *silently repeat,* "God bless you. I love you, peace. Be still."[5] Alternatively, you can assert any part of this statement that best applies in the moment.

I learned these "nine magic words" from John-Roger many years ago and have used them hundreds of times with great results. I have used them in professional meetings, with upset staff members, clients, friends, and family members, and with myself.

What I do is very simple. While listening to any outer discussion, I silently say these phrases in any order for a few minutes, directing the loving, peace, and blessings to the upset party or parties. If nothing else, my inner repetition helps *me* stay calm and centered. Often it seems that this acts like a nurturing balm, and within a few minutes, everyone involved is calmer. Tensions gently melt away and solutions come forward with greater ease.

I once shared this technique over a telephone crisis line with the mother of an emotionally disturbed teen. Several weeks later, the family's therapist called to thank me, as the mother found it one of the most useful strategies she had ever received from a counselor.

Are you starting to feel less at the mercy of your ee-motions? You are not trying to control them, but by observing them, you may find they have less power over you. As you observe and accept your ego energy in motion, you will see patterns more clearly, and you will have more choices. Journal about your experiences with these strategies.

CHAPTER 18

Mirror, Mirror

I commit myself to a process of self-loving.

I first did this mirror exercise in 1979 after a workshop led by a traveling team of facilitators at the University Church of Religious Science in Las Vegas. I do not recall the name of the group, but I have deeply appreciated their work and shared it often with clients along the way! At the end of the workshop, along with about two hundred other people, I committed to look myself in the eyes each morning for thirty days in a row and tell myself, "I love you."

For me, week one was easy. I stared into my reflected eyes and said, "I love you," almost as a rote exercise. The second week I felt my normal persona crumbling. I cringed as I looked in the mirror, as every unlovable thing about myself—every stupid error and ungenerous thought—floated to the surface of my mind. I did not want to stand in front of that mirror and tell myself, "I love you." I wanted to hide my face in shame! But I continued because I had made a commitment. After another ten days or so, negative feelings lessened, and I felt surges of warmth, joy, and hope as I expressed love for myself.

At the end of the thirty days, I loved my mirror sessions! With tears of gratitude and appreciation, I overflowed with love for my own sweet self. This life-changing awareness profoundly deepened my inner awakening. I was more in touch with my spiritual guidance. I enjoyed longer periods of inner peace and acceptance for myself even as I stumbled and bumbled through challenges. Over the years I've repeated this mirror work twice with greater ease but with deeper self-loving.

Since many of my students struggled with low self-worth, I shared this technique with classes as a possible self-nurturing strategy. Many students experimented, reporting powerful emotional results. One memorable young woman waltzed into class, dramatically dropped her self-nurturing paper on my desk, and joyfully caroled, "I learned to love myself!" Her paper reflected consistent work with self-loving statements in front of her mirror and a radical shift in her self-compassion and self-esteem. She glowed.

Another student reported that his low self-esteem climbed five points mainly because of saying into the mirror, "I love you." He missed a few days and started over twice, so he continued the process beyond the term paper deadline. His presence in class shifted from almost invisible in the back of the room to quiet, thoughtful participation, and his face changed from blank to animated.

How to Nurture Yourself with a Mirror and Calendar

This mirror approach is deceptively short and simple. It takes about a minute a day. Read these instructions and contemplate what is involved. Then make a commitment in writing to complete at least thirty days of this process. (A thirty-five or forty-day schedule is preferable.) Put a check mark or sticker on a calendar each day to keep track of your progress. If you miss a day, start over from the beginning and complete your commitment for your chosen consecutive days.

Commitment to the Mirror Process

I, _____, commit myself to a process of self-loving. For the next ____ days, I will look into my own eyes in the mirror, say my name, and tell myself, "I love you." If I miss a day, I will start over at day one and continue until I complete ____ days in a row.

Signed_____

Date_____

Simply Loving You

While looking into your eyes in a mirror, say your name and assert, "I love you." Take a few seconds to *look deeply* into your eyes as you say the words.

Do this every day to complete your commitment. Consistency is extremely important in letting your unconscious self learn to trust the conscious you as you assimilate the sincerity and truth of your love.

What If You Don't Feel Loving?

You may find that when you look in the mirror, instead of loving or liking yourself, you actually hate, dislike, or judge yourself. If so, you may use a few approaches. You could seek professional help with your emotional well-being. You could simply love the part of you that hates you! After all, it's just another part of you. You could practice self-forgiveness daily along with your mirror work, beginning with statements, such as, "I forgive myself for judging myself as hating myself. I forgive myself for judging myself as not ready for my own love." Alternatively, you could postpone the mirror exercise until you complete significant self-forgiveness.

Or you could go ahead and express your loving anyway! *Just do the process.* Say the words consistently day after day and see what unfolds.

Regardless of any negative emotions, you are bigger than any part that *hates* yourself. You are bigger than any negative feelings or memories that arise.

From that larger you, which *is* unconditional loving, even if it does not *feel* real, express your love to your whole self. Simply observe—yes, go back to your neutral loving observer please!—whatever emotions or unloving memories pop up and let them be. Focus on stating your name and saying, "I love you."

Do this day after day so the message can sink in. Some people find it helpful to say, "I love you anyway."

Rate Your Level of Self-Loving

Expanding the role of the neutral loving observer, you might also want to rate your level of self-loving daily during this process. You might start at zero self-loving, and by the end of thirty-five days, you may move up to a three. In that case, you might choose to do another round! Or you might start by thinking you love yourself very well already, maybe first rating yourself an eight, and find that you dip down as hidden judgments surface and then soar to a ten or more. Journaling about your process would also be helpful.

When I start rating a quality to track my progress with an intention, my process is simple. I determine that a five is "normal for me at this time," and I rate myself up or down from there as applicable.

CHAPTER 19

Nurturing Your SMART Parts

*Love all of you, even aspects of your personality that you
do not like, that you judge as inappropriate or lacking,
or that you have tried desperately to deny or ignore.*

Developing my SMART Parts Approach

In 1987, as a graduate student at the University of Santa
Monica, I had an assignment to create my own counseling
theory. I had worked extensively with myself by using
techniques of the imagination and having inner dialogues
with a cast of characters who represented various aspects of
my personality. I saw these as wise aspects of myself, serving
valuable functions, even though they typically characterized
my inner conflicts. I developed my first simple-minded
awareness and restoration therapy or SMART parts theory.

I took a *simple-minded* approach, acknowledging these
aspects of myself. Rather than analyzing, I accepted them
as they showed up in my imagination, childlike, cartoonish,
or whatever. Imaginative dialogues with my inner players

brought useful new *awareness*. *Restoration* occurred as parts transformed themselves, renewing my sense of harmony, balance, or self-integration. *Therapy* simply meant using this process for my learning and growth.

Over more than twenty-five years, the process gradually evolved into my current SMART parts work. This is my take on how we create some dynamic personality aspects and how we can transform them if we wish. Look at this section as a practical approach to understanding, nurturing, and transforming any aspects of your personality that have previously caused problems or sabotaged some of your best efforts.

How You Created Your SMART Parts

When you were a kid, stuff happened. Parents yelled or hit, glared or gave the silent treatment, ordered time-outs, or took away toys and privileges—all in the name of teaching you how to be an effective human being. Mostly, they were acting with good intentions, but they had many perceptual filters in place. They were a little like horses wearing blinders, seeing only a narrow slice of reality based on their own life experiences and beliefs. I deeply believe that they were doing their best according to how they understood things.

But let's get back to the fact that stuff happens. When you were a little person surrounded by big people telling you no or how wrong or stupid you were, you probably didn't like it. Or maybe the big people tried to be your friends but failed to provide useful rules or boundaries, so you have never been really sure of what works in dealing with others. Perhaps a part of you felt lost and did not like that approach either.

With the unconscious coping skills of your two- or five- or eight-year-old self, you started making survival decisions. For some of you, it really was life and death, but for many others, it was about how to survive emotionally. Your "little kid" self—some people call this the basic self, and Freud called it the id—did not understand why parents did what they did. Your "little kid" self just knew, "This hurts a lot," so it unconsciously and automatically created ways of coping with whatever triggered the uncomfortable ego energy in motion. It created survival mechanisms.

Survival Mechanism Aspect Rescue Traits

SMART now stands for survival mechanism aspect rescue traits.

According to my current simple-minded approach, you *unconsciously* developed a team of SMART parts or personality aspects to help you cope. As a *survival mechanism*, you developed an *aspect* of yourself to *rescue* yourself by displaying a new personality *trait*.

Maybe one of your SMART parts helped you to hide or to become invisible to avoid criticism. Maybe you learned to be a joker, clowning to diffuse tension and win approving laughter. Maybe you learned to rebel, always fighting back, or perhaps you became stoic, hiding your emotions. Or you tried to do everything perfectly to stay out of trouble. Perhaps you found that being sick got you sympathy and loving attention, or you had to take what you wanted when you could grab it because no one gave to you. You may have expressed yourself as a daredevil or wallflower. You may have been irresponsible or overly conscientious, spendthrift, or frugal. Maybe you disowned or tried to deny some part of yourself, walling off its energy because of a deep hurt or fear, creating a SMART part in hiding. Many "SMART parts" possibilities exist.

If you can identify a personality aspect that challenges you today, you may work with it as a SMART part.

Be clear that you adopted these personality traits to protect yourself from emotional discomfort when you did not have conscious tools for understanding and managing your emotions. You unconsciously created a new facet of yourself, a new personality aspect or SMART part. Together, some of these SMART parts became your emotional emergency response team.

Each SMART part means well, but at age twenty or fifty-five, you may still be reacting automatically based on your inner five-year-old's rescue system. Many of us are still using childhood tactics with little success. The good news is that by nurturing SMART parts, you can transform old reactive behaviors into responses that match your current needs.

Nurturing Your SMART Parts

Whatever personality aspects you may have developed or disowned, it is more valuable to provide loving and nurturing to them than to understand them intellectually. Rather than seeking analysis or explanations, focus more on restoring wholeness and harmonious functioning in your personality. Here is a very specific example of my own work with a SMART part.

Loving Hidey

As a psychotherapist, I used my SMART parts approach with a number of clients, but then I returned to social work and did little direct therapy. I forgot this strategy for a few years until I immersed myself in studies leading to my doctorate in spiritual science.

At one point I stalled for a few months on writing the practical treatise (original research paper) required to graduate. Reflecting inwardly, counseling myself, I discovered a part of me who identified herself as Hidey. In my imagination she looked like an old-fashioned Swiss storybook girl. I could see her name was Hidey, not Heidi. (My subconscious mind loves puns!)

I remembered my previous SMART parts work, but instead of conducting an extensive dialogue with Hidey, I made a point to spend two or three minutes each evening lovingly speaking to this character. Although Hidey expressed fear of completing the paper and being more visible in the world, I made no effort to change her. I just told her how much I loved her.

After about ten days of loving Hidey, my spiritual advisors showed up as clear inner images along with Hidey. Hidey ran over to sit on the lap of one of the advisors. He asked her, "Where do you belong ... really?" She pointed to me and *whooshed* across the imaginary room to meld back into me.

Although I had almost given up on finishing the practical treatise, three days later I woke from a powerful dream with renewed energy to complete my doctoral work. I met my deadlines and graduated as planned.

This work bypasses the intellect and can be quite magical if you have a little patience, persistence, and the willingness to experiment as you extend love and caring to key fragmented aspects of your personality.

SMART parts self-nurturing approaches are not for everyone, but if this option appeals to you, it can unlock some stuck places in your consciousness. If you happen to be involved in psychotherapy or life coaching, you might want to incorporate these processes into your work in the resolution of personal issues. For me, having an imaginary character represent the habitual but outdated protective response pattern provides quick access to awareness and often leads to healthy change without a need for formal psychotherapy.

Step by Step: Nurturing a SMART Part

In order to do this work the first time, set aside twenty to thirty minutes, and keep your journal handy. Create a peaceful environment so that you are not disturbed. Read these directions ahead of time, and be sure you understand them. A short reminder list at the end of this section can easily lead you through the process.

Light for the Highest Good

Get quiet. According to your faith, you might set an intention or say a prayer, including asking for clarity, understanding, and transformation ... in the light for the highest good.

Identify an Aspect or Challenging Area

Select a personality aspect or life area where you would like more clarity and freedom. Hold this gently in mind. Don't be too attached to it because your inner wisdom may bring something else into your awareness instead. I strongly suggest working with just one SMART part at a time.

Imagine a Special Place

Imagine a special, sacred room or a beautiful outdoor scene where you are perfectly safe, protected, and peaceful. Take a moment to become fully present, and savor the sweetness of this inner sanctuary. Go ahead and notice the details you see, feel, or hear. If your inner sacred space is simply a blank or a void, this is fine too! You may simply know or intend that you are in a special inner place.

Become the Neutral Loving Observer

Become your neutral loving observer, observing with caring and compassion.

Ask Inside

Ask inwardly to meet with an aspect of yourself (a SMART part) related to your interest for today. When it shows up, you may see or hear it, or you may just know or feel that a specific part of you is present. When this part shows up, it might look or sound like a movie character, or it may seem like yourself at a younger age. It could be a cartoon figure, someone you like or dislike, or some other representation of yourself. It could be invisible. Sometimes inanimate objects appear, but typically, they can communicate in some way.

Get Acquainted

Go ahead and get acquainted with this SMART part of yourself. As silly as it may feel at first, just chat in your imagination as if you were talking with a new friend. If your mind wanders, you fall asleep, or you can't easily focus on a dialogue in your mind, try speaking out loud. Or write down the dialogue as it occurs just like you would in a movie script. You could write, "Me," and jot down your comments or questions. On the next line, write the name of the SMART part and whatever it says in turn.

Converse with Open-Ended Questions

As you get acquainted, rather than looking for yes or no answers, ask open-ended questions that require detailed, specific answers. *Would you tell me about yourself? Who are you, and what do you do inside of me? How do you help me?* Whatever answers you get, follow up with questions asking for more details as you wish. You want to *invite* this part to communicate with you.

Embrace and Love Your SMART Part

After a bit of acknowledging or getting acquainted with your SMART Part, simply tell it, "I love you just as you are. You are a wonderful part of me, and I am grateful for your assistance all these years." Or you can express similar words that fit best for you.

When I am using this approach, I do not try to correct, change, or negotiate with this part of myself. I do not move into old emotions or judgments. I just love this SMART part as one element of the multidimensional, multifaceted package that is me.

Repeat Daily

Your first session may take about thirty minutes from start to finish, including journal notes.

Later sessions can last only two or three minutes at bedtime or some other quiet moment in your routine. Repeat this process daily for a week or two until your inner experience changes, indicating some sort of integration or transformation is taking place.

Be faithful to this practice! You are creating a trusting relationship with your SMART part. This work is deceptively simple but powerful. *Consistent* application of loving is a big key for success.

As your ongoing sessions focus mainly on telling your SMART part how much you love and appreciate it, you can then become the neutral loving observer. When you acknowledge and nurture this aspect of yourself, you may note that your awareness opens up, you gain new understanding, or your patterns of thought and behavior provide new revelations.

Document Your Process

Write a brief note in your journal detailing what you learned after each session. A line or two may be plenty. Or just give yourself a sticker or a mark in your digital reminder list. Keep track of your daily participation and any learning you receive.

Loving the Inner Enemy

Your inner sabotage expert, which may show up as the quitter, the one who throws tantrums, or the overspender, among others, is just another SMART part doing its best to help you out but using some outmoded techniques. Identifying and loving your inner enemy may seem like a radical approach. It seems counterintuitive to love an aspect of self that you have judged harshly. Your instinct may be to ignore and forget about this "worst enemy" personality aspect.

In the New American Standard Bible, Luke 6:27–28 quotes Jesus as saying, "Love your enemies, do good to those who hate you, bless those who curse you, pray for those who mistreat you." What if you applied biblical wisdom to your *inner* self?

Yes, you can love whatever aspect you perceive as the enemy within and watch transformation unfold.

Love all of yourself, even aspects of your personality that you do not like, parts that you judge as inappropriate or lacking or that you have tried desperately to deny or ignore. If you are willing to embrace, nurture, reclaim, and restore these disowned parts of yourself, you will be more whole and complete, and you will likely feel more energetic, effective, authentic, and happy.

Here are two more examples of how this process works.

Loving Grumpy

For many years I unconsciously hid and ignored an aspect of myself related to anger. The pattern originated when I was three. One afternoon I angered my dad, and he spanked me. In tearful, passionate three-year-old defiance, I declared, "I hate you!" He chased me through the house, caught me by the cedar bush outside, and spanked me again, towering over me, glowering, and yelling, "Don't you ever say that again!"

Based on how I expressed myself after that, I must have instantly concluded that showing anger was *not safe*. A SMART part took root to help me hide and deny anger whenever possible.

As a normally quiet and mellow adult, I habitually ignored small irritations, especially from my husband, mindlessly popping them into some unconscious compartment to simmer. Weeks or months later, unpredictably, something would bug me, and I would erupt in anger way out of proportion to the aggravating event.

Working with myself some years ago and inviting my imagination to assist, I encountered a Disney-style dwarf who introduced himself as Grumpy. This was the anger I had not wanted to acknowledge since I was three years old! I began the work of loving Grumpy for a couple of minutes each evening. In a few days, he simply quit showing up as a character and had reintegrated into my overall personality.

Suddenly, without any conscious effort, I found I could express my grumpiness with people. My husband was sure surprised! No more bottling up my emotions and exploding like a volcano at unexpected moments. No, sir. If he was grumpy with me, I could be grumpy right back in the moment.

Did this cause more arguments? Not really. We started to have more discussions, most of which were triggered by one of us becoming irritated or concerned. We learned to deal with conflicts, annoyances, and hurt feelings at a much lower level of emotional intensity. We can now usually grump and talk without a full-blown argument, harsh words, or hurt feelings.

Loving the Ski Dude

An executive laid off in a major company reorganization unsuccessfully sought a new job for two years. He felt quite discouraged. Learning of my technique, he contacted a part of himself that he had walled off after a romantic disappointment in college. At first, this SMART part was unseen, hiding behind a high brick wall, but the executive expressed his loving and caring through the wall. The next day this younger version of him was out on skis and saying, "Hey, dude." After three more days of loving his inner ski dude, this man flew on family business and chatted with his seatmate, a business owner. Seeing how his skills could transfer to her field, she immediately hired him as a consultant. A few months later, he joined her executive staff full-time, moved his family across the country, bought a mountainside home, and became the dude on skis (at least on weekends).

Please let me know about your experiences with this strategy by sharing your testimonials on my blog at www. IlenyaMarrin.com!

Checklist for Working with SMART Parts

1. Intend or request light for the highest good.
2. Identify an aspect or challenging area of your life.
3. Imagine a special, safe place for a meeting.
4. Become your neutral loving observer.
5. Ask inwardly to meet a SMART part.
6. Get acquainted. Converse with open-ended questions.
7. Embrace and love your SMART part. Repeat, "I love you just as you are."
8. Document your process.
9. Repeat daily until a positive shift occurs.

CHAPTER 20

Self-Forgiveness: Moving Deeper

It is not the situation itself but what you tell yourself you don't like about the situation that upsets you.

Moving Deeper

The following material is adapted from a handout I created and have used for years with clients and students. Please return to this material as needed to build a solid foundation of self-forgiveness.

Identify the Self-Judgments

When you are feel guilty, ashamed, or generally upset or out of balance, stop for a nurturing moment. Become the neutral loving observer. Look at the situation plus your thoughts and feelings. What negative thoughts or self-righteous beliefs are triggering your upset feelings?

Subtle clues to self-judgments show up in your language. Consider the times when you think or say, "I should— I shouldn't— I must— I have to— I ought to—" Likewise, when you criticize yourself or say, "I'm *too* this or that," "I can't," or, "I'm not enough," you can trace that impulse back to an irrational belief and sneaky judgment. (See chapter 15 for more about how to transform your language patterns.)

If you have experienced harm and now feel hurt, anger, fear, shame, or betrayal, gently unearth the related self-judgments. What specifically are you telling yourself that contributes to your feelings? Listen for any self-judgment in your words.

For example, watch for words like, "They shouldn't have— This isn't fair." At this point you seem to be judging *them* or the situation. Maybe the situation is indeed not fair, but is anyone *forcing you* to be upset? Not likely. Your *judgments* are making you upset. It is not the situation itself but what you tell yourself that you don't like about the situation that upsets you. Using the previous example, you might decide that your underlying discomfort has arisen because you feel out of control or because you believe that people *should* have acted differently than they just did.

Choose Self-Forgiveness

Start with whatever self-judgment you identify right now, and forgive yourself. "I forgive myself for—" Continue forgiving yourself until you experience a clear shift to a much lighter, more positive, and more loving emotional energy. Here are a few examples.

Forgive Things You Did

"I forgive myself *for* being angry with myself. I forgive myself *for* not asking for what I really wanted and needed. I forgive myself *for* breaking the vase." Often that is enough, and I am able to release any self-judgments in the moment.

Forgive Value Judgments

"I forgive myself *for judging myself as* a victim. I forgive myself *for judging myself as* speaking when I shouldn't." I learned at USM that many self-judgments, such as calling yourself names or criticizing your personality qualities, fall into the emotion-laden category of value judgments.

To continue with the example of the vase, if I continue to dwell on the accident or feel stuck in negative emotions, I switch to forgiveness of the value judgments. "I forgive myself *for judging myself as* clumsy. I forgive myself *for judging myself as* not paying attention. I forgive myself *for judging myself as* needing to replace the vase. I forgive myself *for judging myself as* stupid!"

As another example, you might say, "I forgive myself *for judging myself as* a failure."

Please note that if you say, "I forgive myself for being a failure," there is an underlying message that you really are a failure! This is not a self-nurturing statement!

On the other hand, saying, "I forgive myself *for judging myself as* a failure," simply implies an error in judgment. This is good.

You want to release the judgment, not wrap more negativity around yourself! That two-letter word "as" is a big key. I suggest you reread this section and let the information sink in thoroughly.

Structuring Your Process

In working with clients new to this process, I note that a few minutes of making statements of self-forgiveness will usually shift their energy from judgmental to compassionate and accepting. They are then free to handle practical problem solving or move ahead with their dreams. Complex or traumatic self-judgments might take longer, or they might be addressed a chunk at a time in shorter sessions.

As you practice, be gentle with yourself. Do as much as feels comfortable in one sitting. Practice a little self-forgiveness daily if possible. For example, for about a year, I checked in with myself for five minutes nightly and forgave any self-judgments that came to mind. This is deeply self-nurturing!

Forgive Yourself Out Loud

As you begin, I encourage you to speak statements of self-forgiveness aloud. You get the double benefit of speaking the words and hearing yourself. If you identify as spiritual, say a prayer in accordance with your faith to request that God assist you. Speaking aloud to God or the divine may help you stay on track.

Another good way to learn self-forgiveness is to write your statements in a journal. The physical act of writing helps you stay focused, grounded and thoughtful as you identify and release each judgment.

You might also make mental statements of self-forgiveness. Because it can be easy to start replaying the problem instead of focusing on the self-forgiveness, I suggest that you use this method only *after* you have some practice making statements out loud or writing them down.

If you want to release self-judgments related to severe trauma, you might seek a skilled practitioner who has done his or her own work with self-forgiveness to support your process.

Follow the Flow

Follow the spontaneous flow of your thoughts and feelings, and make statements of self-forgiveness about whatever comes to mind. If tears arise, be gentle and compassionate with yourself, but keep going!

Perceptions of Others

Forgive yourself for judging yourself through the perceptions of others. Often, self-forgiveness for your current situation will lead to awareness of related self-judgments or times when you took on judgments from others in your life—parents, teachers, and so forth.

For example, if someone often said to you, "You're dumb," you may tell yourself words to that effect now. In effect, you are still judging yourself through the viewpoint of that parent, spouse, child, teacher, etc. Saying, "I forgive myself for *judging myself as dumb through the perceptions of my brother*," can help unlock and release that specific pattern in your consciousness.

Judging Others

Forgive yourself for what you judge in another. This is more radical, and for most people it is counterintuitive. You'll be practicing *ownership* of your entire experience in a profound process. *What you own you can transform inwardly.*

Let's say you judge a friend as arrogant and feel mildly victimized by his attitude, but you can't figure out how to forgive yourself because you are not judging yourself. First, see what happens if you simply say, "I forgive John for being arrogant." If you release the judgments, great.

If you continue to feel resentful or disturbed, try making statements such as, "I forgive myself for judging *myself* as arrogant." In a free-flowing process, compassionately forgive *yourself* for every little thing you are judging about that other person. You might find interesting new self-awareness. Note any shifts in your emotions. Next time you see John, notice any shifts in the interactions.

I like using this approach when I get upset with the people closest to me. For instance, if I see that I am judging my husband as too outrageous in his playfulness, I do not even bother with "forgiving him." He is just being himself. I'm the one with the attitude problem. Here is a sample of my inner dialogue if and when I flip to forgiving myself for being too outrageous.

> **Me:** I forgive myself for judging myself as too, too outrageous! I forgive myself for judging myself as overstepping the bounds of propriety! I forgive myself for judging myself as socially insensitive.

> **NLO in Me:** Hmmm. So there is a part of me that really knows how to overstep boundaries and social niceties. There's also another part of me that really likes to be in control, not only of myself but of the whole social scene around me!

> **Me:** I forgive myself for judging myself as out of control. *Sigh of relief.*

> **NLO in Me:** I caught the energy shift, the sigh of relief with that last forgiveness. Okay, when I forgive myself for judging myself as out of control, it is easier to accept that he is just being himself, and that is okay. It is not a reflection on me.

> **Me:** The judgment on him just evaporated along with my forgiveness of me.

Resisting Self-Forgiveness

You might find yourself wanting to avoid or resist self-forgiveness because you believe that it will be complex or emotionally messy or that you will have to relive an awful experience. You might think that forgiving yourself would make you irresponsible, that you need to continue to suffer with guilt and shame, or that you are unforgivable.

These beliefs will keep you stuck in pain or denial. Forgive yourself anyway. Yes, emotional discomfort may surface as you acknowledge and forgive past judgments, but repeating self-forgiveness can bring gradual shifts and then a release that is truly freeing and self-nurturing.

This process does not excuse accountability. If you need to make amends, do so. I will talk a little later about forgiving others who may have harmed you, but remember, it is important to forgive yourself first.

The Self-Forgiveness Habit

Get in the habit of forgiving yourself for little judgments. Recently, I walked through a doorway, but my shoulder didn't quite make the turn. Ouch. Immediately, I said, "I forgive myself for judging myself as clumsy." I rubbed my shoulder for a moment and went on.

My husband and I once chided an older friend for giving us poor directions to the home where she was staying as a guest. This tiny, white-haired lady instantly declared with gusto, "I forgive myself!" Not only was she not judging herself, but she was not taking on our judgments either!

These instant responses come after lots of practice. If you begin by practicing self-forgiveness in relatively minor situations like the ones I just described, you will create a great habit, stop the buildup of self-judgments, and be more comfortable when you tackle a larger issue.

Saying the Words, Peeling the Onion

At times it may seem you are simply saying the words. But if you keep saying the words, sincerely practicing this process, at some point you are likely to feel a distinct shift, a sense of relief and weight being lifted. The world will look lighter and brighter. I have often felt I was "peeling the onion," revisiting certain issues over the years, and lifting many layers of residual judgments before finally completing the release.

Repeat Often

One of the most nurturing things you can offer yourself is self-forgiveness and compassion. Make it a habit to forgive yourself as often as necessary to lift the layers of judgment. When you release self-judging thoughts, your emotions flow into more positive expressions. You clear out old beliefs standing between you and your awareness of your innermost loving self. Use self-forgiveness often to stay clear in the moment, or in longer, more focused sessions for profound personal healing and sacred inner realignment. Your experience will be more telling than any of my words. Then celebrate the freedom in your authentic, worthy, loving self.

For additional thoughts on self-forgiveness as well as many other tools for living as your authentic self, I highly recommend the book *Loyalty to Your Soul: The Heart of Spiritual Psychology* by Drs. Ron and Mary Hulnick.

Forgiving Others

In the first example of self-forgiveness in chapter 8, my friend was clearly a victim of child abuse. Those events helped shape his life and the expression of his personality for years. In our phone call, he verbally forgave his mother for what she did and his father for what he neglected to do.

More importantly, he forgave himself for judging himself as someone who did not know how to protect himself or escape, unable to control the situation. He forgave himself for judging himself as a victim. In doing so, he removed the negative emotional charge from his memories. He moved into inner peace with more compassion for his parents and their struggles as well as for himself and his medical issue.

Major Upset, Big Self-Forgiveness

This example from my own history describes my only *marathon* of self-forgiveness. Many years ago a body worker made some unexpected changes to my musculature. At home in front of a mirror, I felt aghast at my instant "Buddha belly," as I had once taken so much pride in my flat abdomen. I had sought help for a different issue. The practitioner had neither asked if I wanted nor prepared me to expect this abdominal change. He did not touch my stomach during the work, and he did not respond to my upset phone calls seeking clarification after the fact. I vented to my husband and a few understanding friends, but I was still extremely upset with the whole situation.

After three days of self-righteous victimhood, I remembered my tool of self-forgiveness. I prayed for light for the highest good and began making statements of self-forgiveness out loud. I forgave myself for judging myself, for choosing this particular body worker, for not asking more questions, and for allowing myself to feel like a victim. I forgave myself for judging myself as someone (perhaps unconsciously) in need of this type of experience. I forgave myself for judging my anger and sense of betrayal.

Somewhere in this litany, I forgave the body worker for whatever came to mind about his approach.

Then my free-form statements branched out even more, and I began forgiving myself for things I might have read in books, seen in movies, or imagined but had never consciously done myself. I forgave myself for judging hundreds of past hurts, disappointments, self-betrayals, and times when I let others down. Sometimes I forgave myself through clenched teeth, and sometimes through tears, but I kept going.

With any thought that popped into my head, I turned it into a statement of self-forgiveness. "I forgive myself for judging myself as a traitor. I forgive myself for judging myself as jumping off the garage roof with my brother and scaring my mother. I forgive myself for judging myself as shooting myself in the foot."

Were these real? Jumping off the garage and terrifying my mom really happened when I was six or seven years old. The others—and many more of that nature—I don't know and don't care. This session became a marathon of sweeping junk from my subconscious mind.

After ninety minutes my energy shifted. I came to a natural stopping place. I felt lighter and much freer inwardly. Objects in my room seemed brighter, more vivid, and clear. I still did not like my bulging belly, but the giant emotional charge had lifted. I experienced an inner relief, a peace with the circumstances. I resolved to suck in and restore my flat abdomen and move on, and over the next few months, I succeeded.

There are a number of books worth reading about how to forgive others when you have experienced harm. However, in working with clients and my own issues, I find the most empowerment from forgiving myself. Forgiveness and acceptance of others seems to come as a bonus.

Yet another perspective asserts that we are all bobbling around in this soup of human consciousness together! When you forgive yourself, you forgive the world.

PART 5

Keep the Change

Roots of Compassion

Keeping the change is like encouraging the roots of a tree to go deep for a lasting foundation. In my yard, I nurture young trees with water and nutrients, remove weeds, and cut off suckers that choke growth. In my life, I bathe in spiritual experiences, foster positive thoughts, and gently release toxic ones. I pay attention to messages from my emotions. I feed, water, and exercise my physical self. With strong roots grounded in self-compassion, I can survive storms and dance beautiful patterns in the winds of change.

Gentle, simple strategies done consistently act as a tonic for your consciousness. They say, "I matter. I am worthy of my own loving and caring attention." When you know that you matter, physical energy quickens, emotional responses settle down, mental awareness clarifies, and spiritual awareness expands. How are you sustaining your tree of life?

CHAPTER 21

Nurturing Your Levels of Consciousness for Personal Transformation

The right way to nurture yourself is your way.

Have you ever done something nice for yourself and felt quite restored as a result? Perhaps you walked for an hour on a beautiful beach or visited your local botanical garden. Maybe you spent twenty minutes in meditation and felt rejuvenated, peaceful, and ready to carry on with your responsibilities. Maybe you listened to an uplifting speaker and let the ideas inspire daring next steps, or you played your favorite music while driving or doing chores. Do you remember the extra energy and good feelings? The clarity and joy?

How often do you do things for yourself that bring feelings of love, appreciation, gratitude, inspiration, or inner peace? How often do you talk kindly to yourself when your day is falling apart?

We all have room to add more self-nurturing experiences to our busy lives. In fact, when we consistently take tiny steps to care for our multidimensional selves, the long-term effects are transformational.

This chapter is about using your existing knowledge and experience to create a gentle self-nurturing plan that supports you right here and now. If you persist in following your plan, experimenting to find the best strategies for your lifestyle and temperament, your "here and now" practices will become an ongoing transformative experience.

Please become a compassionate research scientist on the most important subject of your life—*you*. Explore and discover how to help yourself grow, blossom, and ascend higher in your personal aspirations. Experiment with planting seeds of heartfelt compassion and practical caring for yourself, and let those seeds grow, bear fruit, and bless others.

The right way to nurture yourself is your way.

Multidimensional Self-Nurturing

Each of us is a whole yet complex being. One useful way to approach self-nurturing is to look at four basic levels of consciousness—physical, emotional, mental, and spiritual. If you do a small self-nurturing strategy on each level, you will be leading all your levels of consciousness forward in a balanced way. Even if you only do one strategy for one level, the change on that level will tend to pull the other levels forward along with it.

In workshops I sometimes create a demonstration by labeling four people with the four levels of consciousness. They line up, holding hands. I tell the person representing the mental level that he or she has been saying positive affirmations for a week, and the person may step forward a few steps. As this person moves a few feet forward, he or she naturally pulls on the hands of participants on either side. With a second week of positive affirmations and a few more steps forward, the people beside the "mental level" person must step forward to keep up. By now even the physical level is starting to move ahead, powerfully illustrating the interconnected nature of consciousness. Whenever a level of consciousness advances because of consistent small steps, the other levels naturally make progress too.

Match Your Lifestyle

Please design your self-nurturing experiments to suit your needs and lifestyle. Plan in terms of small, simple changes that will fit realistically into your daily routine. Post reminders where you will see and heed them. Be gentle with yourself. Be consistent. Set up some simple method of keeping track of your progress. Rather than giving up if you miss a day or two, keep coming back to promising strategies.

Possible Strategies

The rest of this chapter is a smorgasbord of ideas that have worked for me and people I know. Use these as a springboard for planning a few of your own strategic gentle steps forward. For help in identifying specific areas for self-nurturing, you might want to complete the Life-Satisfaction Assessment at the end of this book.

Here are some questions to help you set your focus. What would let you know you are taking good care of yourself? What gentle steps could you take to feel inwardly nurtured and cherished by yourself? What would help you remember you are worthy of your own deep love?

On the physical level, you can do anything that helps your body feel and function better. What do you enjoy? Walking, running, swimming, gardening, and/or playing a sport? Well, maybe at first you do not relish the thought of a run, but you know that afterward you feel so wonderful! Feeling happily satisfied is key, especially if you have not been physically active for a while.

Some people motivate themselves to workout simply because they love the results. Meeting a friend for a swim three mornings a week could be very nurturing. If one of these scenarios fits for you, go for it! I seem to need the motivation of walking our greyhounds to nurture all of us. I do feel better afterward, but not enough that I would walk twice a day without the happy dances by McMan and Too Cool Cathi! Set it up so you enjoy it!

Other strategies on the physical level could be as simple as drinking two big glasses of water to rehydrate first thing in the morning. Go to bed earlier, and log more sleep time. Increase your fruit and veggie intake. Eliminate sugary drinks or diet sodas. What have you *wanted* to do for yourself because you suspect it would be very good for you?

This is not a time to haul out a long list of *shoulds*.

I recommend very gentle, small changes. Cut out that bedtime cookie habit, not because you want to deprive yourself but because you will sleep better without the last-minute carbs and sugar revving up your system.

Experiment. Make one change for a few weeks and see what happens. If you like the results, keep doing it. If your process was working well but you fall off your track, simply start over. Be the neutral loving observer, and notice what tends to undermine your self-nurturing efforts. Make adjustments accordingly. You might decide to nurture a resisting SMART part following the directions in chapter 19.

On the emotional level, look for things that help you feel happy, joyful, loving, enthusiastic, confident, and peaceful. At this point we start to have overlap between the emotional, mental, and spiritual strategies.

Traditional ideas to nurture your emotional level of consciousness include listening to uplifting music, taking a bubble bath, or looking in the mirror and telling yourself, "I love you." (See the "mirror, mirror" strategy in chapter 18.)

You could work with self-forgiveness (chapter 8), love a SMART part (chapter 19), or enter statements of gratitude in your journal daily. Some physical-level activities such as dance really boost mood. Anger management and stress reduction techniques could also fit in this category along with dozens of other gentle self-nurturing steps. What would help you feel better emotionally? How can you apply love and care to aspects of you that most need tender encouragement?

On the mental level, you have lots of room to experiment. Stating affirmations (chapter14), changing your story (chapter 13), listing daily successes, and managing your time are candidates for this level. Meditation (chapter 10), self-forgiveness (chapter 8), or nurturing a SMART part (chapter 19) could also be mental level strategies.

Personalize your experimental strategy. What small area of thinking or speaking could you tweak with consistent practice? Maybe you have a habit of saying any challenge that arises is "a pain in the neck." Make a point to drop that phrase and instead say something like, "This is an opportunity to observe, learn, and grow." One such simple change may well alert you to other habitual language patterns so that you naturally start changing those to the positive as well. Observe how your ee-motions behave when you persist in changing your language. Perhaps you are not as irritated, or maybe you feel more peaceful and centered.

Reading an uplifting page a day can help shift mental patterns. Some people find uplifting quotes on the Internet for daily inspiration or subscribe to a joke a day. Journal writing is deeply nurturing for many. Others like writing and burning letters to ventilate or release nagging thoughts. Writing statements of gratitude or listing your next steps toward achieving your heart's desires could be mental level strategies to nurture yourself forward.

On the spiritual level, what would help you connect with the joy of spirit? With your inner wisdom? With your loving spiritual self? Inspirational reading, uplifting audio or video material, services or lectures, prayer, meditation, contemplation, reflection, and journal writing are all possibilities.

Perhaps you have learned specific strategies in previous workshops but set them aside in the bustle of daily life. Rejuvenate these practices and let them rejuvenate you from the inside out! Even five minutes devoted to devotion can trigger transformative inner shifts in your awareness. For starters, you could tell yourself, "I am willing. I make time, and I am learning to nurture my spirit."

Watch for More Great Strategies for Nurturing You

Be alert for strategies on any level of consciousness that appeal to you and that you could gently and easily incorporate into your routine. For instance, I often do five squats or shoulder stretches while I'm drying my hair or waiting for my vitamin C drink to finish fizzing.

You may find keys to explore in books or magazines, on the Internet or television, or in a chat with friends. Watch for small game changers that spark your interest and a feeling that makes you say to yourself, "That might be good for me!" Write it down! Snap a photo of the instructions. Get your friend to show you how. Practice as soon as you can. Check it out. If you are still enthusiastic, consider whether you could commit to doing this activity daily for a week or a month. If yes, put it on your tracking list and get started. Note your results.

If you make a habit of checking out self-nurturing ideas, in a few months you might have experimented with fifteen or twenty new strategies, and you may have found three or four keepers that work well for you.

I am suggesting small, easy steps. Get that bottle of Vitamin D3 and put it where you will see and take it each morning. Write D3 on your calendar when you swallow. Be the NLO. Make occasional journal notes about any health improvements.

Tailor Self-Nurturing to Your Lifestyle

Tailor strategies to your lifestyle. For instance, if your schedule does not permit workouts at the gym, what kind of workout could you set up in your bedroom? Pull out old magazines or look online for suggestions and create a doable twenty-minute routine—a bit of stretching, a few squats, a few push-ups, and three or four more simple moves you always meant to try. Rather than complaining, "I can never find time for the gym," you will be doing something positive for your physical self!

Set your emotional energy for the day. For a minute before you do your makeup, look in your own eyes and say, "I love you." Listen to upbeat music on your commute so that you can arrive at your job with sparkle, and turn on peaceful music when you are coming home to unwind from a stressful day and recharge for your family or personal evening.

Repeat your affirmations at stoplights or in the restroom. Sing them to yourself as you drive, or speak them while you walk. Put your journal on your pillow or wherever you savor your morning coffee. During the day, jot down good questions to ask yourself for journal exploration or write snippets of awareness to expand on when you have a few minutes with pen in hand.

Keep uplifting reading on your bedside table for the morning or evening. Create your own peaceful sanctuary with a cozy chair and table, a candle in a beautiful and safe holder, and your favorite aids to meditation or prayer. Practice meditating for five minutes at a time while the kids play at the park or you sit in a waiting room.

Nurturing Yourself First to Overcome Specific Issues

Consider various areas of your life. Where do you feel dissatisfied? (If you need ideas, check the Life Satisfaction Assessment at the end of this book.) Pick an area you want to transform. What self-nurturing strategy could you apply to gently, compassionately shift that area to satisfaction?

Last year I started using an over-the-counter mouth guard to stop grinding my teeth at night. Immediately, each morning my neck and shoulders felt more relaxed. A few months later, as chiropractors had suggested for thirty years, I could sleep with a roll-shaped pillow supporting my neck. Until I used the mouth guard, I could never tolerate that lump of pillow! My chiropractor has commented that I have a nicely curving neck now, and my neck and shoulder tension continues to improve. It takes ten seconds to insert the mouth guard and another ten to pop the pillow in place. This is basic, gentle self-nurturing with long-term payoffs. I keep doing it because I like the results.

As another example, a painfully shy woman said hello to one stranger the first day and gradually built up to speaking to ten strangers a day. She held herself at that level for five weeks, successfully overcoming her shyness.

One mom in her late thirties took her kids to karate and thought it looked so fun she signed up too. Without dieting, she dropped forty pounds in six months.

A middle-aged woman practiced kindly but firmly saying no to rides and loans for mooching relatives until they quit pestering and she had time to study and care for herself.

Several students with financial woes began tracking their spending, setting aside savings, and paying off debts. The resulting peace of mind was both nurturing and empowering!

Once a week a woman dons headphones, tunes into opera on the radio, and builds intricate dollhouses and furniture. Another comes home from a demanding job and unwinds by creating pen and ink sketches before cooking dinner. Creativity is wonderfully self-nurturing!

A young woman who never spent time with her horse scheduled riding and grooming time three days a week. Her health, grades, and relationship immediately improved because she so enjoyed being with her horse!

One woman writes love notes to herself and leaves them near her journal to read in moments when she needs a boost.

Numerous students of various faiths happily reconnected with church, temple, or mosque attendance, or they made time for prayer and scripture reading. Many made a regular practice of meditating for a few minutes daily, reporting wonderful inner peace and increased ability to manage their stressful lives.

Nurture Yourself First in a Relationship

Looking for a relationship? What are the top qualities you would treasure in a mate? As an example, if you say *honesty* and *caring*, then become ruthlessly honest with yourself and with others, nurturing that quality until you know you are trustworthy inside and out. Be impeccably caring with yourself, saying no to downer social obligations and events with negative acquaintances. Nurture yourself the way you would want your mate to nurture you. Give yourself the love, respect, and freedom you want from a partner. You may find you meet a partner with exactly the qualities you are nurturing in yourself.

Visit my blog, www.IlenyaMarrin.com for longer lists of potential strategies you could apply to each level of consciousness.

Creating Your Personal Experiment

Whether you will do best with one or two self-nurturing strategies or you are bursting to take on a dozen, only you know! Listen to your heart and your gut.

Choose enough to let yourself know you are in the game of self-nurturing. But keep it doable. I would prefer to see you do less and go slowly than take on too much and have one more burnout experience in the name of self-nurturing.

If you tend toward Superwoman heroics, create a very small, easy self-nurturing experiment. Use anything that I have suggested or that you have dreamt up, but take only one or two simple steps. Give yourself permission to be yourself with no pressures for ten minutes a day. *Show up faithfully for your low-key strategy.* When you are satisfied with the first experiment, declare it complete. Continue to use any strategy that has proved itself especially useful. Choose one or two more small steps for your next experiment. Keep going.

If you are often frustrated because you do not challenge yourself enough or you have a specific issue that self-nurturing might resolve, you could create a more complex experiment dealing with several levels of consciousness or areas of life. Like my students, you could do one or two small changes in each level of consciousness—physical, emotional, mental, spiritual, financial, or creative. Again, keep it doable, and feel free to simplify and tweak your process so it works for you.

Your Inner Freedom Uplifts the World

Are you sensing how these gentle, experimental steps can free energy and create space in your consciousness? With inner freedom comes more wisdom and joy, more resilience and empowerment to exercise your heartfelt loving as an individual connected with billions of other caring souls.

As you take basic steps to nurture yourself, you live in greater balance. As you care for yourself, you emerge into a field of living love with more to share. You naturally lift those nearby, joining in heart-centered action that ultimately uplifts our world.

CHAPTER 22

A Self-Nurturing Lifestyle

More than being just okay, nurturing yourself first is essential for effective living in our complex world.

How do you keep the change? How can you continue the nurturing and maintain a gentle, ongoing process of personal transformation? What would keeping the change mean for you? How can you continue to reap the harvest of your own nurturing? What would help you endure as a practical spiritual scientist, observing your adventures with neutral acceptance and compassion?

For most people not motivated by a grade on a term paper, the hardest part about self-nurturing is establishing a consistent routine of self-care. In this section, you will find some ways to make the routine easier.

For me, self-nurturing has never been a quick fix. It is a lifestyle. Keeping the change means being faithful to myself and my process of learning. It means gradually growing, and unfolding with greater loving. It means cutting myself slack and yet holding to my purpose of gently, naturally caring for myself. It includes a profound and loving commitment to my own innermost self and the multidimensional package that I call me.

Nurturing Endurance

When you consistently take small steps, you keep moving forward to success. You gain both inner and outer rewards and enjoy the satisfaction of a goal completed or a quality manifested. The following thoughts might help to keep your self-nurturing experiment working at optimum levels.

Ask Good Questions

When you ask yourself practical questions, you indicate you are willing and open to positive change. When you are willing, the how-to part appears. In order to keep moving forward with your chosen small steps, you might make a habit to ask yourself questions along the following lines:

- What's going on?
- How am I doing? Is this process still working for me? If not, what are my alternatives?
- How could I tweak my process, adjust my thinking, soothe my emotions, redirect my actions, or dig deeper in Spirit?
- What is being shown to me right now?
- What can I learn from this situation?
- How can I see or approach this differently?

- How can I use this to learn, grow, and uplift my consciousness?
- How can I use this to nurture and care for myself more fully?

Consistency: Keeping Priorities on Your Radar

When my main self-nurturing practice was twenty minutes of meditation twice a day, I simply made it a priority and did it at my preferred times. I felt so good after each session that I was happy to defer other activities for those few minutes. Today, with too many self-nurturing practices to commit to memory, my best tool for keeping them all on my radar is a simple chart with room for checkmarks, brief notes, or stickers. With my printed chart, half the work is done before I start. All I have to do is show up and mark the page.

I recommend that you start with between two and five self-nurturing practices. You might use your existing day planner, a wall calendar, the chart I provide, or make a spreadsheet of your own. Acknowledge each bit of progress. Use colored pens or stickers on a calendar. One friend made giant calendar pages on poster board and used large stickers for fun and exciting visual proof of her daily successes. Another friend uses colorful code letters on a small calendar. If she meets her goals, she gives herself a smiley sticker at the end of the month. Keep your tracking process simple and enjoyable so you will do it.

Remember, you are not committing forever to your specific strategies, but you want to give them a fair trial. Commit for five weeks. Then evaluate your progress, and decide what to change. Aim to be consistent yet flexible. If they work well, you have the beginnings of a new habit.

You will probably enjoy keeping a written record of self-nurturing activities for the following reasons:

- Whatever format you choose, the list itself serves as a reminder of your specific intentions for self-nurturing.
- A log or chart helps you stay consistent with practices that have proven effective.
- It helps you stay accountable to yourself on two levels, as a neutral loving observer and as the participant in your own experiment.
- One- or two-word notes can capture progress, wins, or challenges to help you evaluate a particular strategy.
- You acknowledge yourself for taking each small step in self-nurturing! Seeing the line of checks or stickers build up is rewarding!

Commitments

I quickly get sloppy when I don't use a tracking system. Without my reminder page, I can easily feel rushed in the morning, think, *I'll do it tonight*, and then let it slip again. My chart keeps me honest in my commitment to nurture myself. Tracking tiny steps helps me build good habits of self-nurturing—habits of the heart.

Why do I check off boxes? This is the easiest way I know to organize and visualize my progress. It is scientific in a simplistic way. I have a record of what I did, and I can observe the results.

For instance, I did a short intention for maintaining youthful appearance for years. I received many compliments on how young I looked, and friends didn't believe my age. Wanting to streamline my morning rituals, I took this intention off my reminder list. Six months later I noticed more wrinkles and fewer disbelieving comments. My intention apparently worked better than I knew! Subjective evidence is better than no evidence. Vanity wins! This item is back on the chart.

Aiming in the Right Direction

Some self-nurturing strategies require a bit of effort, such as carving out time for yourself from your overbooked schedule. How can you balance the needs of your personal or inner self with the needs of your professional self, and your role as spouse and/or parent?

I have worked with these principles long enough to know that my inner self is ultimately more important than any of the outer roles that I play. It is so easy to get caught up in outer activities, busy work, and social obligations. Yet I still have to remind myself that my inner self needs time and nurturing. Spiritual exercises are my bottom-line practice, even if I only have five minutes on days when I start driving at 6:30 a.m. Some mornings I wake up tired and make a deal with myself that I'll go to bed early tonight. Some nights I am better at sticking to this agreement than others, but I am listening to my needs and aiming in the desired direction.

Inner Rewards

Keeping the change means reinforcing my positive behavior. Usually I don't need tangible rewards. I need the inner rewards of self-respect and integrity when I hold steady with my process and I know I can trust myself. But I am gentle with myself when I do not stick with the process. I am flexible and know I can get back on track. I can do this. I think I can. I can keep coming back to the positive over and over again no matter how many times I might eat those lovely, crunchy, salty corn chips and gain two pounds overnight!

Beyond Willpower

I need to go beyond willing myself through the tasks I set. I need a habit of loving myself enough to keep on loving myself. What pulls me forward into the greater being that I am? I have always felt a drive to learn about myself, to improve myself, to be a better person. I am called forward to be all I can be.

My spiritual exercises are foundational, for they nurture the core of my being, my soul, my connection with God. They help me stay peaceful and loving. Also, exercising acceptance and compassion for myself and for others helps me sustain self-nurturing.

When I remember that I am doing the best I know how with what I have to work with—and so is everyone else—I am the neutral loving observer compassionately watching and learning. With learning and new awareness comes new growth. I transform myself through loving.

You also can find gentle, transformative steps that nurture you in the specific ways you need right now. Be willing to explore this process or way of life called self-nurturing. Put on your "neutral loving observer" hat and discover what works for you. What makes you feel more centered, balanced, and resilient? What helps you remember that you are a spiritual being having a human experience? What helps you take good care of your body and treat your mind and emotions with love and respect? What enables you to encourage and inspire yourself? What is fun and uplifting?

Remember, nurturing yourself *first* is essential for effective living in our increasingly complex world.

CHAPTER 23

Self-Nurturing Circles

Sharing struggles and successes provides
touchstones for your transformative growth.

Keeping the change is about loving yourself and aiming for your highest purpose, answering the call of your authentic self as best as you can. You might find that when you take a few steps forward in self-nurturing, some previous pain backs off. If your motivation was mainly to alleviate stress or a painful challenge, when you temporarily stop hurting, your determination fades, and action fizzles. How can you stay motivated to maintain your nurturing strategies?

My introductory psychology students were highly motivated by their assignment for a five-week project plus a term paper. They earned an outer reward, specifically a significant grade, for getting briefly but deeply engaged in personal transformation. Furthermore, I repeatedly focused on the value of self-awareness and shifting consciousness through lectures and discussions, encouraging students to relate concepts to their own lifelong learning.

Motivating Yourself

How can you create motivation for ongoing self-nurturing? Support from other people can help you stay focused and on track.

In my early years of self-nurturing, I learned largely from friends, occasional counseling, and many classes and workshops. Now I am in two support groups, one related to my spiritual growth. I meet weekly by phone with three other women scattered across the country, and we read and discuss a bit of John-Roger's work. We also cherish and uplift one another. The other group is based on Julia Cameron's book, *The Artist's Way.* I meet with writers, artists, performers, and other imaginative folks to support my creative process.

Even though I am an introvert, I find social support invaluable. For most people, support of like-minded friends or colleagues is essential in sustaining personal transformation. As long as all parties share similar goals, it does not seem to matter whether that support appears on an individual basis with a trusted friend, counselor, or coach, or in some class or group format. Sharing struggles and successes provides touchstones for your transformative growth. Mastermind groups, prayer partners, support groups, twelve-step groups, *Artist's Way* groups, and many others may contribute to self-nurturing and sustaining change for healthier, happier, more creative, and more successful living.

How to Create a Self-Nurturing Circle

If you want to create a self-nurturing group, the following suggestions can help you begin. If you come up with useful exercises, formats, or wonderful outcomes from participating in such a group, please share your stories with me at www. IlenyaMarrin.com!

Ultimately, create your group in whatever way best nurtures you and the other group members. These are guidelines to help you get started.

- Keep it small and simple. Two to six members might be ideal. It may be better to have smaller groups of three or four who can meet consistently rather than one bigger group with many members missing at times because of scheduling conflicts.
- Set aside the time and stick to it. Sixty to ninety minutes should be plenty of time for a group of two to six.
- Have a clear purpose. For instance, your mission statement may say, "We are here to support one another in nurturing ourselves." If you feel you are getting off track, come back to your statement of purpose.
- Have some sort of opening, perhaps a prayer according to your faith or a statement of intention and group purpose.
- Commit to participating for a specific time, such as twelve weeks. At the end, look at the needs of the group and decide whether and how to continue. Maybe someone drops out, and you open the group to a few new members at this point. Or you may change

the meeting time to accommodate members' changing schedules.

- Be on time. If you are each on the phone or meeting at someone's home, keep distractions from children, pets, and other sources of background noise to a minimum.
- If ending on time is important, rotate functioning as timekeeper to be sure each person has time to share.
- For the meeting format, use this or another book with a focus on self-care or transformational growth to help set your theme. You could all read a chapter or a few pages in the book each week prior to the meeting and then briefly discuss what you each learned from the reading or what it means to you. Then share about your experience of self-nurturing for the past week. What were your commitments to yourself? What did you do that worked? Be the neutral loving observer for one another and for yourself.
- Let each one have uninterrupted time to talk. Give feedback only if the speaker requests it.
- When someone else is speaking, really listen with your heart. Tune in deeply to what he or she is saying. If and when the person asks for feedback, you might first check out your impressions with the speaker to be sure you understand. Are you hearing him or her accurately? Then share your ideas.
- Acknowledge and praise small steps in the direction of self-nurturing, self-discovery, and self-transformation. Often a group member might not realize how much she is doing right to nurture herself until you point it out. Encourage more self-compassion, self-forgiveness, and self-acceptance.

- Let go of judgments. In feedback portions of the group, you could remind one another to release judgments by saying, "I forgive myself for judging myself as—" If speakers request feedback, share your ideas on what they might be able to do differently. Avoid giving advice or telling other people what to do! Instead, stick to sharing what has worked for you, or offer possibilities for them to consider. A very open way to do this is to say, "If I were dealing with that, I might—" Or you could say, "When I handled a similar situation, I did—" Or you might offer two or three possible suggestions so that people are free to choose. Speak to group members with the caring you would like others to extend to you.

PART 6

Be the Change

*Extend your personal empowerment to broader circles
as you are called forward into an age of living love.*

CHAPTER 24

Nurture Yourself and Change the World

As a result of your self-nurturing, your family is steadier, your community a bit more balanced, and the ripples expand. Your world, which is our world, is forever shifted to a more loving one.

Global Awakening

We, the people of earth, are waking up. We connect intimately with one another through the breath of life and the spiritual essence that enlivens us and expresses itself through us as love, care, and generosity. Some of us are still walking through a nightmare of violence, terrorism, and war, acting out the remnants of old patterns of dominance and control. Like any nightmares, these will subside in the light of awakening.

We can assist with global awakening by doing a few simple things.

- We can love and care for ourselves first and give from the overflow to one another.

- We can discover who we are in our authentic essence as individuals and as deeply connected human beings.
- We can make decisions not based on fear but centered in loving intention for the highest good of all, including ourselves.

Common Perspectives

I recently gave a talk on self-nurturing to a small group of women in a private home. These were caring mothers and grandmothers concerned about family and community issues. I asked what they would think if I said that by nurturing yourself, you could change the world. With glazed disbelief, they shook their heads. They could not see how this was possible. They did not seem to feel they had permission to take care of themselves at deep levels. My question did not even fit within their current worldview.

Sharing casually with a young dental hygienist, I heard a different perspective related to self-nurturing. She knew she needed to take better care of herself, but between work and family responsibilities, where would she find the time? She also felt uneasy about the state of our nation. "I don't know who to listen to, who to trust. I'm scared for my children." The uncertainty of national politics and world conflicts heightened tensions around her personal challenges.

A brilliant college student said her acquaintances needed help in finding their voices and being true to themselves. She was concerned that they were selling out "who they really are, who they could become" for the security of a boyfriend and hope of marriage. This young friend sees herself as being in a process of self-discovery, learning who she is, and defining who she will become. She wants to nurture herself more fully in order to fulfill her potential.

Some of you may be like the women in these examples. You long to nurture yourself because you need to refill your own cup. You give so much and handle so many stressors that you need to take better care of yourself so that you can continue to be of assistance to those closest to you. But beyond that, you wonder, "How could I possibly affect the world?"

Women everywhere are the caretakers and culture-keepers for the people. We pass our wisdom through our families, our work, and our communities. In the Western world, we are so individualized and so isolated within small family units that we often forget how we do comprise a larger cultural or collective consciousness.

Yes, of course, men can participate in this, but I have addressed women in this book because so many women have been trained to ignore their own needs and care for others first. Many wonderful men find it easy and natural to take care of themselves first and then give to others. Most women need this message more than most men do.

Permission for Self-Nurturing

What if we begin giving ourselves full permission to take care of ourselves first so that we may give from our overflow to help take care of others? To manage ourselves and our family responsibilities, to nurture partners and children, and to contribute to our communities from a full, rich, heart-centered space within?

What if we take care of ourselves so well that we truly know who we are as spiritual beings having a human experience on earth and that we need not react with anxiety to the daily news? What if we find that self-nurturing and self-compassion lead to deep resilience, the ability to bounce back and remain balanced in the face of stressors? What if we find others who care for themselves as valuable and valued beings and we connect with them to achieve goals beyond our individual powers?

When you nurture yourself, you make the most of yourself from the inside out. You treat yourself like your own best friend. You are the author of your experience, the creator of your screenplay. When you rewrite it from a perspective of taking good care of yourself, you can reap both inner and outer rewards, and the effects of your loving consciousness spread more widely than you might imagine.

Contract for Learning on Planet Earth?

Imagine if you will that you made a spiritual contract before you were born to learn and grow in this amazing school called Earth. You entered this world with a curriculum to master certain life lessons. You picked family members and other key players plus helpful or challenging life circumstances to nudge you into achieving those goals.

A similar perspective simply says that many factors contribute to the multidimensional package that walks around in your skin, the consciousness that you experience as you—genetics, unconscious memories, immediate personal experiences, your culture, other people, media, and environmental factors. At some level you are choosing to participate with all of this.

What shifts in perspective occur when you try on these ideas?

When I think of life this way, I feel empowered rather than subject to the mercy of fate. If I had a role in choosing my life plan, my meanderings don't seem random. I can see major themes in the lesson plan of my life. I willingly nurture myself because I see how I bounce back and learn from the challenges of my life curriculum more easily when I care for myself with compassion.

Can the idea that you somehow helped to choose your life circumstances assist you in taking better care of yourself?

I think we are evolving to a new form of the human race because of rapid cultural and environmental change. We have agreed to master our life lessons in the midst of global changes in weather, technology, pharmacology, politics, and more, some of which impact us right down to the cellular level. Circumstances are encouraging us to make new choices for thriving as spiritually centered, authentic and loving human beings, so it behooves us to make the most of what is present.

What is your role in changing your own consciousness and thereby helping to change the consciousness of the world?

The Ripple Effect

When you nurture yourself, you change. Giving more love to yourself, you have more to give to others. You are more in touch with your intuitive wisdom, more resilient in face of challenges, more resourceful in finding loving solutions, and more instrumental in making the impossible possible.

As you nurture yourself and connect with others who are nurturing themselves, it is easy to pour the overflow of love, wisdom, and creativity into efforts for the common good—help for the local school, the elderly, or an organic community garden. It is natural to hear the song of love in others and to recognize that beyond diverse races, faiths and factions, we are all part of a body of love. It is easier to cooperate on a larger scale, supporting the song of love in all beings. As a result of your self-nurturing, your family is steadier, your community a bit more balanced, and the ripples expand. Your world, which is our world, is forever shifted into a more loving one.

You will not automatically be a perfected being because you start taking a weekly bubble bath, doing yoga three times a week, and writing statements of gratitude at bedtime. But you may well have more patience with your kids and find the energy to be on a PTA committee where you make a difference in your child's school. You may chat with a couple of friends and encourage them to take better care of themselves. Maybe you create a small support group by phone once a week, or you meet at a coffee shop.

We women need to learn that it is highly desirable to nurture and care for ourselves. Stress levels on the planet are rising.

Only when we take care of ourselves can we continue to assist our loved ones and be energetic players in our communities. Only when we keep our individual cups full and overflowing can we give without depleting ourselves. With consistent self-nurturing, we give from the heart-centered abundance of our true selves.

If we start with ourselves, the rest will grow organically. I had a lot of work to do to bring balance within myself before I was ready to share beyond a very small group. Wherever we are as individuals in self-nurturing and in our creative expression, we are in the perfect space for this time and place. We simply start nurturing ourselves where we are planted and allow more inner wisdom to come present and lead us to our next steps. According to our faith, according to the song of love within, we move, grow, and share with others.

Together, we can change the world.

END MATTER

Endnotes

1. John-Roger, *Fulfilling Your Spiritual Promise*, vol. 1, p. 5.
2. Neff, K., "Self-Compassion vs. Self-Esteem." http://www.self-compassion.org/what-is-self-compassion/self-compassion-versus-self-esteem.html. Accessed June 24, 2014.
3. John-Roger with Paul Kaye, *Living the Spiritual Principles of Health and Well-Being*, p. 163.
4. John-Roger and Paul Kaye, *Momentum: Letting Love Lead*, p. 25.
5. John-Roger, *Loving Each Day for Peacemakers*, p. 100.
6. John-Roger, *Spiritual Warrior: The Art of Spiritual Living*, pp. 89–91.

Bibliography

John-Roger. *Fulfilling Your Spiritual Promise*, vol. 1. Los Angeles: Mandeville Press, 2006.

Allan Richards, "How to Become a Spiritual Warrior?" an interview with John-Roger, *New Millennium*, Oct/Nov. 1998.

John-Roger. *Loving Each Day for Peacemakers*. Los Angeles: Mandeville Press, 2002.

John-Roger and Paul Kaye. *Momentum: Letting Love Lead*. Los Angeles: Mandeville Press, 2003.

John-Roger. *Spiritual Warrior, The Art of Spiritual Living*. Los Angeles: Mandeville Press, 1998.

Kristin Neff, "Self-Compassion versus Self-Esteem." Accessed June 24, 2014. *http://www.self-compassion.org/what-is-self-compassion/self-compassion-versus-self-esteem.html*.

Math Chart: Ripples of Self-Nurturing

Year	Potential Self-Nurturers										Grand Total
1	4										
2	16	4									
3	64	16	4								
4	256	64	16	4							
5	1,024	256	64	16	4						
6	4,096	1024	256	64	16	4					
7	16,384	4096	1,024	256	64	16	4				
8	65,536	16,384	4,096	1024	256	64	16	4			
9	262,144	65,536	16,384	4,096	1,024	256	64	16	4		
10	1,048,576	262,144	65,536	16,384	4,096	1,024	256	64	16	4	
Total	1,398,100	349,524	87,380	21,844	5,460	1,364	340	84	20	4	1,864,120

Spiritual Exercises

After about ten years of meditating, I discovered the Movement of Spiritual Inner Awareness and shifted to their practice called spiritual exercises (SEs). I switched with an inner sense of rightness, but I remained open to the possibility that if I found something to take me higher, I would follow it. Here I am, thirty years later, still doing SEs with deepest gratitude.

In case this appeals to some readers, I wanted to share this format. Since spiritual exercises are a very specific form of meditation, I am quoting with permission the following section from John-Roger's book, *Spiritual Warrior: The Art of Spiritual Living.*[6]

Tool of the Spiritual Warrior

Spiritual exercises (SEs) are designed to help us break through the illusions of the lower levels and move into an increased awareness of the Soul. Doing SEs is an active technique of bypassing the mind and emotions by using a spiritual tone to connect to the energy that flows from God.

The only wrong way to do SEs is not to do them, so there are no rules, rituals, or postures that are necessary to begin your practice. SEs are an action of the heart, in which the approach is one of devotion and a clear intention to know Spirit and God in a greater way.

Having said that, for those people who would like to have some form of methodology so they can begin their SEs, here is a step-by-step procedure as a suggestion for doing fifteen minutes of SEs.

1. Find a quiet place with low lighting and a comfortable chair to sit in. It is best not to listen to music while doing SEs.
2. Sit upright, and close your eyes.
3. Say a brief prayer asking for the Light of the Holy Spirit for the highest good, and ask for protection and guidance during your SEs.
4. Chant the Hu (pronounced h-u or hue) or the Ani-Hu (ah-nigh-hue), which are sacred names of God. It is preferable to do this silently.
5. While chanting, focus your attention in the area near the center of your head directly back from your forehead. It is in this place that the Soul has its seat and the Soul energy gathers.
6. After you have chanted for about five minutes, stop and listen within. You are listening for the sound current, the sound of a vibration of God, which is very subtle. You may hear it the first time you do this, or it may take years of practice. It is very individual.
7. If you find your mind wandering and you lose the focus of listening, you can focus the mind by chanting again.
8. After about five minutes of listening, you can either continue to listen and look inside or return to chanting again. The idea is to spend time in SEs both chanting and listening.

9. If you see the color purple coming from the right or center of your head, you can allow yourself to follow this inwardly, for this is a form the energy from the highest source of Light and sound takes when it is awakening people to an awareness of their Soul. This is known as the Mystical Traveler Consciousness. If the color is coming from the left side, we advise not following it because this is often a negative influence. (All this applies to seeing inwardly.)

10. After about five minutes more, you can open your eyes. You may want to wiggle your fingers and toes to bring the energy back into your physical body.

So ends your fifteen-minute session of SEs. Through daily practice, you can gradually build on this time period until you reach the recommended time of two hours a day. For longer periods of SEs, you can expand the time for chanting and listening to fifteen minutes each. For example, in an hour session of SEs, you can chant for fifteen minutes, listen for fifteen minutes, and then repeat the chanting-and-listening cycle one more time.

All of the above are guidelines, and it is important to remember that the only wrong way to do SEs is not to do them. So you can experiment with how you do SEs, using what works for you a particular time and not getting too attached to a certain form. And, again, the focus is on doing your spiritual exercises with as much loving and devotion to God as you can.

Life Satisfaction Assessment

Rate your satisfaction level on a scale of one through ten. One is extremely low or nonexistent, and ten is extremely high or completely. This rating will make you think about many different areas of your life, so you have several options to consider when you decide on your gentle self-nurturing practices.

This list is certainly not all-inclusive. If you have other areas of importance, write them in the blank spaces and rate them. If you know a specific subarea that's challenging for you, make a note of it. If an area doesn't apply, leave it blank or write N/A.

Please note that this is not a scientifically validated questionnaire. I created it to give you a snapshot in time of your satisfaction levels today. There is no right or wrong way to answer. You are simply looking as a neutral loving observer and assessing your satisfaction level for now. Check again in a few months or next year, and reflect on what is changing and why.

Life Areas that Might Include Challenges or Opportunities for Growth	Satisfaction Level 1–10 rating
Study and college success skills	
Parenting	
Relationship with another	
Relationship with yourself	
Emotions (anger, depression, anxiety, shyness, etc.)	
Memory	
Confidence or courage	
Habit patterns (positive or negative routines, etc.)	
Addictions (smoking, drinking, drugs, sex, food, shopping, etc.)	
Time management	
Money management	
Being responsible/accountable	
Being yourself (authenticity)	
Self-trust (self-honesty)	
Ability to do neutral, scientific observation	
Spiritual faith	
Physical health	
Mental health	
Emotional well-being	
Stress management	
Self-esteem	

Life Areas that Might Include Challenges or Opportunities for Growth	Satisfaction Level 1–10 rating
Self-compassion and self-nurturing	
Self-forgiveness and self-acceptance	
Work	
Sports or recreation	
Understanding dreams (from sleep time)	
Fulfilling a personal dream or goal	
Sense of purpose and direction	
Creativity	
Financial well-being	
Add Additional Areas to Rate Below	

Tracking Chart Example and Template

Here is a sample tracking chart with a few items filled, in followed by a blank template that you may copy. Or you can visit my blog, www.IlenyaMarrin.com/tracking, and print out the larger chart found there.

To use this tracking page, you would fill in items you want to observe, similar to the example page. Then you would either check off a box meaning, "Yes, I did it," or fill in a number such as ounces of water, number of hours/minutes, exercise repetitions, and so forth.

You could also rate any positive quality or intention on a one-to-ten scale. I normally declare that a one is very low, that a ten is very high, and that five means "normal or average for me at this time." Then I intuitively rate myself up or down according to the experience of the day.

On a larger chart, you can use stickers to mark progress. You may find apps for your phone with similar formats and use those, or you can use a household calendar and colored markers to track your progress.

	Sample Tracking Chart							
	Dates							
		M	T	W	Th	F	S	S
1	Water (ounces)	58	54	64	64	50	64	64
2	Hours of sleep	5	6	6	5	6	9	8
3	Inner peace rating	5	6	5	4*	6	6	6
4	Meditation-minutes	7	10	10	-	10	-	5
5	Mirror Mirror	x	x	x	x	x	x	x
6	Energy rating	6	6	6	6	6	7	7
7								
8								
9								
10								
11								
12								
13								
14	Argued with Joe							
15								

Tracking Chart

Dates								
		M	T	W	Th	F	S	S
1								
2								
3								
4								
5								
6								
7								
8								
9								
10								
11								
12								
13								
14								
15								

Book Club Questions

1. How does this author's approach differ from that of your mother or grandmother? How does self-nurturing fit into a contemporary lifestyle? Is it practical? Is it necessary?
2. Do you already nurture yourself? Or do you spend much of your time and energy looking after others? If so, how do you nurture yourself? If not, what might you begin to do differently?
3. Does the phrase "Nurture yourself" leave you feeling guilty or selfish? Is it worth changing your outlook to be more accepting of good self-care? What personal and social challenges will you have to overcome to be more nurturing of yourself?
4. How would life change if many of us became neutral loving observers? How would your life change if you adopted this perspective?
5. How would your life be different if you did not criticize or judge yourself?
6. Is self-judgment necessary to be a good person?
7. What did you hope to gain by reading this book? What practical tools have you gained, and what changes in awareness have you experienced? Which tools will likely be most useful? How can you continue a focus on self-nurturing?

8. How aware are you of your multidimensional levels of consciousness (physical, emotional, mental, and spiritual) and your need to care for each of those levels?

9. How does our culture promote or allow self-nurturing? How does it impede self-care?

10. Do men need to nurture themselves? If so, how? How could you share self-nurturing tools with key men in your life?

11. How could you teach your children to nurture and care for themselves? In what ways are you modeling or demonstrating self-nurturing now?

12. How will nurturing you assist others in your home, work, and community environments?

13. What could you do to promote better self-care for yourself and others in your sphere of influence?

14. How can self-nurturing create greater self-compassion, resilience, and access to heart-centered wisdom? In what ways might self-nurturing contribute to a more loving world?

15. Is personal and planetary transformation possible? Is it desirable?

Suggested Reading

Here are a few books that serve as resources for me. Many other fine books and authors can contribute to your journey of self-nurturing. Dive in and enjoy!

- *You Can Heal Your Life* by Louise L. Hay
- *Loyalty to Your Soul: The Heart of Spiritual Psychology* by H. Ronald Hulnick, PhD, and Mary R. Hulnick, PhD
- *The Artist's Way: A Spiritual Path to Higher Creativity* by Julia Cameron
- *The Game of Life and How to Play It* by Florence Scovel Shinn
- *Open Your Mind to Receive* by Catherine Ponder
- *Living the Spiritual Principles of Health and Well-Being* by John-Roger, DSS, with Paul Kaye, DSS
- *Spiritual Warrior: The Art of Spiritual Living* by John-Roger, DSS
- *Momentum: Letting Love Lead* by John-Roger, DSS, with Paul Kaye, DSS
- *Fulfilling Your Spiritual Promise* by John-Roger, DSS
- *The Blessings Already Are* by John Morton
- *You Are the Blessings: Meditations and Reflections on Life, God and Us* by John Morton

Did you enjoy *Nurture Yourself First for a Change*?

**Claim your free list of
100 Gentle Ways to Nurture Yourself !
Visit my website,**

www.IlenyaMarrin.com.

Click on Send My Free List!

Printed in the United States
By Bookmasters